A TEACHER'S GUIDE TO
change

We dedicate this book to the teachers who volunteered to tell us about their experiences with change. Their thoughtfulness and candor, even when recounting experiences that had been painful, brought this book to life. We are in their debt.

A TEACHER'S GUIDE TO
change

Understanding,
Navigating,
and Leading
the Process

Jan Stivers
Sharon F. Cramer

CORWIN
A SAGE Company

For information:

Corwin
A SAGE Company
2455 Teller Road
Thousand Oaks, California 91320
(800) 233-9936
Fax: (800) 417-2466
www.corwinpress.com

SAGE Ltd.
1 Oliver's Yard
55 City Road
London EC1Y 1SP
United Kingdom

SAGE India Pvt. Ltd.
B 1/I 1 Mohan Cooperative
  Industrial Area
Mathura Road, New Delhi 110 044
India

SAGE Asia-Pacific Pte. Ltd.
33 Pekin Street #02-01
Far East Square
Singapore 048763

Printed in the United States of America.

Library of Congress Cataloging-in-Publication Data

Stivers, Janet L.
A teacher's guide to change : understanding, navigating, and leading the process / Janet L. Stivers, Sharon F. Cramer.
    p. cm.
Includes bibliographical references and index.
ISBN 978-1-4129-6446-3 (cloth)
ISBN 978-1-4129-6447-0 (pbk.)
    1. Teachers—In-service training. 2. Change (Psychology) I. Cramer, Sharon F. II. Title.

LB1731.S717 2009
370.71'55—dc22   2009014370

This book is printed on acid-free paper.

09   10   11   12   13   10 9 8 7 6 5 4 3 2 1

Acquisitions Editor:	David Chao
Editorial Assistant:	Brynn Saito
Production Editor:	Amy Schroller
Copy Editor:	Claire Larson
Typesetter:	C&M Digitals (P) Ltd.
Proofreader:	Carole Quandt
Indexer:	Sheila Bodell
Cover Designer:	Scott Van Atta

Contents

Preface

With middle age on the horizon, Ross decides he must leave the small private preschool where he has taught, and thrived, for 12 years, to accept a position with higher pay and a pension plan at a large public elementary school.

After 23 years teaching sixth grade in the town's middle school, and with only one year to retirement, Sally is transferred to the primary school to teach second grade, where there is an enrollment bulge.

Michael is preparing for his tenure year when the only other fourth-grade teacher in his building becomes seriously ill. With grave misgivings, Michael agrees to the principal's request that he take over his colleague's inclusive class and coteaching responsibilities.

The high school English department's preview of new state assessments leads them to conclude they must revamp the curriculum to emphasize works of nonfiction. Janice, whose third child is a toddler experiencing developmental delays, is distressed when she realizes she will spend most of the year teaching from books and assigning projects she has never used before.

Teacher preparation programs ground teachers in learning theory, curriculum development, instructional strategies, assessment techniques, and any number of concepts and skills needed to teach effectively. But they appear not to address one topic common to all teachers' experiences: change. How do teachers learn to meet the many changes that they will face throughout their careers? How do they learn to avoid the burnout that can result from failure to adapt to change? How can they become energized, rather than defeated, by unexpected change? How can they seek out change as a means to transform themselves, their classrooms, schools, and communities?

We have written *A Teacher's Guide to Change* to prepare K–12 classroom teachers to understand, anticipate, and respond creatively to a range of changes teachers typically encounter throughout their careers. Some changes may seem minor, such as adopting new instructional materials or teaching a new grade level; others are momentous in their scope and consequences, such as the large-scale changes in assessment practices that accompanied the No Child Left Behind Act. Regardless of the magnitude, when teachers must struggle to adapt to change, the passions that brought them into the profession can be dampened. We hope to help teachers see change as a choice they can make to enhance their effectiveness and career satisfaction. Because change offers challenge, it also offers opportunities for stimulation and growth. This book has been designed as one that can reconnect teachers to the passion and excitement that drew them to teaching in the first place. Our hope is that our readers will recommit to staying in the teaching profession because they know they can meet the challenge of change, and because they see that openness to change gives them access to professional development opportunities throughout their careers.

It is our intention to provide teachers with practical skills—conceptual, reflective, interpersonal, and strategic—to use immediately as well as in the future. These skills can be used by teachers to adjust to changes that are imposed on them and to changes they choose, as well as to lead others to adopt the changes they champion. Teachers who understand and can manage their responses to change and influence the responses of students, families, and colleagues are more likely to become respected peer leaders and to find satisfaction in a long career in teaching.

When this topic is addressed in research and books pertaining to K–12 education, it is typically directed toward administrators rather than classroom teachers. This book is aimed at teachers and argues that change is not something that merely happens to teachers or must be imposed on them; change is something teachers can understand, manage, become increasingly invested in, and lead. Our intent is to contribute to an increased professionalism of teaching by helping teachers not only understand the change process but also acquire the skills to manage it.

A Teacher's Guide to Change calls on two key sources: the research literature on change management, and the responses of over 100 teachers to a survey about their experiences with change. The quantitative survey questions are presented in Appendix A, along with the results to the fixed response items; responses to the open-ended questions which are not included in Appendix A have been incorporated as examples throughout the book. The teachers who were asked to complete the survey were nominated by higher education faculty because they were thoughtful, experienced individuals who were likely to provide careful and complete responses to a lengthy online survey. We did not seek out teachers with any other special characteristics. From June through December 2007, about 150 teachers were invited to complete the survey; 121 responded and 107 completed the anonymous survey. They had taught all across the United States, as well as in some foreign countries, though most were from the Northeast. They had experience in urban, suburban, and rural schools, and in public, private, religious-affiliated, and charter schools. They taught in general education and special education, at the preschool, elementary and secondary levels. Approximately 20% volunteered to be interviewed at length; the interview questions appear as Appendix B. Since all participants were assured that their anonymity would be protected, pseudonyms are used throughout this book.

A note about quotations and vignettes: We are grateful beyond measure to the teachers who told us their stories. Whenever possible, we have used their own words, editing with the lightest touch and only as needed to achieve clarity; these contributions are indicated throughout the book by quotation marks. Sometimes the teachers described their experiences with change at length, in exchanges that resembled comfortable conversations more than formal interviews; these have become vignettes in our book. Because we had to adapt these accounts for the printed page, they are presented without quotation marks. For a few vignettes, we have recounted experiences from our days as classroom teachers or from the tales told by teachers who once were our students and now are our friends. All of the quotations and vignettes represent authentic experiences of teachers.

A Teacher's Guide to Change comprises ten chapters organized into five parts:

Part I, Experiencing Change helps teachers examine the many facets of a change experience. In Chapter 1, we consider why change is so challenging for most teachers, and why it is helpful to try to face it with confidence and optimism. In Chapter 2, we draw on the experiences of the teachers who responded to our survey to describe, and then ask teachers to look ahead to, the kinds of changes, at school and at home, they might experience that are likely to have an impact on their teaching. In Chapter 3, we explore three dimensions of change—voluntary versus mandated, top-down versus bottom-up, and incremental versus fundamental—and ask teachers to analyze their experiences with change in terms of these dimensions.

In *Part II, Understanding the Change Process*, we take a close look at what usually happens as people experience change. Chapter 4 describes how people typically respond when they first contemplate change, with special attention paid to the phenomenon of resistance to change. Chapter 5 outlines two models of the change process: the stages-of-concern model (self, task, and impact) described by Fuller and Brown (1975) and later adapted by Hall and Hord (2001, 2006); and the transition model (endings, the neutral zone, and new beginnings) described by Bridges (2004). In both chapters, teachers are prompted to look back on changes they have experienced to better understand the concepts and processes presented.

Part III, Implementing Change, describes the steps teachers can take to initiate and carry out a change effort in their classrooms. Chapter 6 helps teachers plan in detail for the undertaking, while Chapter 7 guides them in a six-step process as they implement the change. Both chapters include several examples of change initiatives undertaken by the teachers in our study.

In *Part IV, Leading Change*, we enable teachers who have learned to plan and implement changes in their own classrooms to lead change in a wider arena. Chapter 8 details the change efforts teachers can lead in their many spheres of influence. Chapter 9 helps teachers appreciate that the teaching skills they have already mastered are the foundation for the leadership skills needed to engage others in a change effort.

In *Part V, Changing Throughout a Teaching Career*, we maintain that change can provide the vitality that is essential to a long and satisfying career in education. Chapter 10 encourages teachers to seek professional development opportunities and to assume new roles (for example, as mentors) as a means of insuring that their careers remain meaningful and joy-filled and that generations of students will reap the benefits of teachers who continually renew themselves and their commitment to the profession.

What this book is not: This is not a book for cheerleaders who see change in a strictly positive light. Nor is it for anyone looking for a "quick fix" for disgruntled teachers. Although it might be the basis of a series of professional development sessions, it is much more than the vehicle for a one-time inservice workshop.

What this book is: Our goal is to offer teachers practical strategies that are grounded in theory and research in an engaging and accessible format. We take a pragmatic approach, offering guidelines that can be generalized to multiple settings and using vivid examples so that teachers reading this book will be able to apply the ideas and strategies directly to their own experiences.

This book is a resource for those teachers who are curious about the many different kinds of change they face and who want to manage the change experience more effectively. The key opportunities the book affords teachers are to (1) learn from the experiences of others, (2) act purposefully when choosing how they will respond to change, and (3) craft their own plans to initiate change.

Acknowledgments

The research project that led to this book had its beginnings in the Northeastern Educational Research Association (NERA), which is a regional unit of the American Educational Research Association (AERA). NERA's annual conference has been the greenhouse for many projects we have undertaken over the past 15 years; our work has matured because of the careful review and thoughtful feedback provided by NERA members. We are grateful to all whose leadership and commitment have made NERA a vibrant organization that nurtures educational researchers, and especially to Phil Archer, Janet Carlson, Dick Clark, Nancy Ellis, Bob Gable, Cheryl Gowie, Barbara Helms, Mary Horan, Gavrielle Levine, Diane Liebert, Bob McMorris, David Moss, Katharyn Nottis, Darlene Perner, Julia Rothenberg, Rolando Santiago, Liora Schmelkin, Steve Sireci, Barbara Wert, Dianne Zager, and Ralph Zalma.

We are grateful to the editorial staff at Corwin for their assistance with every phase of manuscript preparation. Early in our discussions, Allyson Sharp made suggestions that greatly facilitated our data collection; throughout the writing process, David Chao offered helpful feedback and direction, as well as support and encouragement; and Brynn Saito provided just the help we needed, just when we needed it most.

We also are grateful to our students, who give our work meaning. Our colleagues at Marist College and Buffalo State College have created an atmosphere where research that benefits K–12 teachers and students is valued and advanced through the give-and-take of collegial discussions. At Marist College, a spirit of goodwill laced with generous doses of humor is sustained by dozens of colleagues, and most notably by Nora Brakas, Jim Dodd, John McAdam, Ed Sagarese, and Dean Margaret Calista. At Buffalo State, colleagues from across campus facilitated this work, including the Institutional Review Board (IRB) approval process (Ted Turkle, Gina Game), research activities (William F. Wieczorek, Sheldon Tetewsky, Kelly S. Marczynski), and the writing and researching process (A. Paul Reynolds, Dennis Ponton).

Most importantly, we thank the friends and family who stuck with us even though we were preoccupied throughout the long process of research and writing: Carly, Kevin, and Mike Stivers; Phyllis Larkin and Bill Larkin III; Andrea Thompson, Rita Silverman, Judy Harkavy, and Pat Backus; Adolph Cramer, Barbara Sears, Joan Weinstein, Gloria Paul, Mary Jo Pfeiffer, Fran Engel, and Samantha Brody. Lastly, both of us were given insights, time, humor, love, and support by our spouses, Dan Stivers and the late Leslie R. Morris, whose belief in us made everything else possible.

Corwin gratefully acknowledges the contributions of the following individuals:

D. Allan Bruner
Science/Math Chair and High School Teacher
Colton High School
Colton, OR

Barbara R. Dowling
Teacher and National Fellow for the Office of Head Start
Sioux Falls Public Schools
Sioux Falls, SD, and Washington, DC

Barbara Glaeser
Associate Professor, Department of Special Education
California State University, Fullerton
Fullerton, CA

Robyn Hilger
Teacher/Program Director
Foundation for Oklahoma City Public Schools
Norman, OK

Karen Kozy-Landress
Speech/Language Pathologist
Brevard County Schools
Merritt Island, FL

J-Petrina McCarty-Puhl
Forensic Science Teacher, Secondary
Nevada State Teacher of the Year
President, Nevada Science Teachers Association
Reno, NV

Ronald W. Poplau
Director of Community Service, Shawnee Mission Northwest High School
Shawnee, KS
Director of Continuing Education, Ottawa University Kansas City
Overland Park, KS

Sharon Redfern
Elementary School Principal, Highland Park Elementary
Lewistown Public Schools
Lewistown, MT

About the Authors

Jan Stivers is Associate Professor of Special Education at Marist College in Poughkeepsie, New York, where she has won awards for excellence in teaching and research five times. Her specialization is helping teachers master instructional strategies that lead to increased achievement for students with disabilities, especially those who are taught in general education classes. She also serves as a consultant to school districts implementing inclusive education, regularly presenting workshops on collaboration and coteaching. Dr. Stivers began her career as a special education teacher and experienced many changes—from teaching in self-contained classes to resource programs to inclusive classes, from middle to elementary and finally to the high school level, sometimes relocating and each time teaching students with different disability classifications and educational needs. These changes were not always welcome, but all eventually proved to be valuable as opportunities for professional growth.

Dr. Stivers was awarded a PhD in educational psychology and statistics from The State University of New York at Albany. In addition to teaching and consulting, she serves on the Board of Directors of Literacy Connections, a nonprofit agency that promotes adult and family literacy in New York's Hudson Valley.

Sharon F. Cramer, PhD, is a Distinguished Service Professor at Buffalo State College, where she has been a member of the Exceptional Education faculty since 1985. Her prior experiences include chairing the Exceptional Education Department and leadership roles in state and national professional organizations, including serving as president of the New York State Federation of the Council for Exceptional Children, president of the Northeast Educational Research Association (NERA) and publications chair of the Division of Developmental Disabilities 1997–2001. In 2003, she received the Burton Blatt Humanitarian Award from the Division of Developmental Disabilities of the Council for Exceptional Children, the highest honor the Division bestows upon its senior members, and in 2008 she was the recipient of the Leo D. Doherty Memorial Award for Outstanding Leadership and Service, the highest award given by the Northeastern Educational Research Association.

Her publications include a 2006 book with Corwin, *The Special Educator's Guide to Collaboration: Improving Relationships with Co-Teachers, Teams and Families,* which is a second edition of *Collaboration: A Success Strategy for Special Educators* (published by Allyn & Bacon in 1998) and "Keys to Successful Collaboration" in M. Lupi & S. Martin (Eds.), *Special Women, Special Leaders: Special Educators and the Challenge of Leadership Roles,* published in 2005 by Peter Lang. She serves as a governance leader, both on her own campus (as chair of the college senate, 2007–10) and on a broader level, as chair of the governance committee of the State University of New York (SUNY) University Faculty Senate (2007–10). Her leadership in the area of enrollment management led to her completion of *Student Information Systems: A Guide to Implementation Success*, a 320-page book published by American Association of Collegiate Registrars and Admissions Officers (AACRAO) in 2005.

A sought-after presenter, Dr. Cramer has given over 100 presentations and keynotes in 22 states and Canada. She completed her PhD studies at New York University, earned an MAT degree from Harvard University and a BA from Tufts University. She has been listed in *Who's Who in America* (60th edition, 2006), *Who's Who in American Education* (2006–present), and *Who's Who in American Women* (62nd edition, 2008). Further information about her can be found at her Web site, www.sharoncramer.com.

PART I

Experiencing Change

The first section of *A Teacher's Guide to Change* explores the many facets of change as teachers experience it. We begin with an overview of how teachers respond to change and consider why it is helpful for teachers to acquire skill and confidence in managing change. In Chapter 2, we draw on the experiences of our survey participants to describe the range of changes teachers experience at school and at home, paying special attention to how these changes affect teachers' work with students. In Chapter 3, we explore some of the dimensions of change, such as whether a change is voluntary or mandated, and ask teachers to analyze their experiences in terms of these dimensions. Teachers' voices are heard throughout this section, to illustrate key ideas and to encourage readers to make connections to their own experiences with change.

CHAPTER 1

Introducing the Challenges of Change for Teachers

*Y*ou'd *think change would be a breeze for teachers.* After all, we are immersed in it. No matter what our content areas or grade levels, we become expert at teaching about change—from tadpoles and caterpillars to evolution and revolution; from change across the global economy to change within the heart of a character; about the lightening pace of technological change and the glacial pace of change when it comes to solving problems like poverty and racism.

More to the point, we spend our days enticing and leading, and sometimes coaxing and pleading with, students to change. We work to help them rethink a problem in light of new information; we try to get them to see a situation from a different point of view. We teach them to use a new procedure and to develop more productive work habits. All of the time, we are trying to help them adopt new critical thinking skills and habits of mind. Ultimately, we aim to enlarge their view of the world and their understanding of their roles in it. Our sense of ourselves as effective teachers derives directly from our ability to help students change—to learn and grow.

You'd think teachers would, in fact, be the natural leaders of change. Experts on educational change such as Michael Fullan and Andy Hargreaves explain that change is, at heart, a learning process; who knows more about learning than teachers? Other educational change researchers describe the ideal change leader as someone who can attend to content and process simultaneously (Havelock & Hamilton, 2004); blending content and process is what teachers do best.

Moreover, we recognize that we have to change even if all we want to do is keep things as they are (Waks, 2007). The forces around us are in constant flux, so to maintain the status quo, we must make continual adjustments, just as we do when trying to keep a car on the road in a high wind. And very often, those adjustments are major. Nearly 90% of the teachers

3

we surveyed[1] said they had experienced a change that had a major positive impact on their lives as teachers, and 70% said those changes occurred at least every three years. They told us about adjusting to change at school, such as teaching a new grade level or content area, adopting new curriculum frameworks or instructional strategies, working with new administrators and colleagues, or moving to a new school. They also told us about how changes in their personal lives affected their performance at school. The good news is that the majority of the teachers we surveyed described these changes as beneficial most of the time, for themselves and for their students.

Despite the pervasive nature of change, and despite our awareness that it usually works out for the best, most of us find change to be difficult. It's easy to see why. Even change that appears minor to others doesn't look that way to us because we know that it will cascade. When we make an apparently small change, like adopting a new textbook, we eventually find that we need something new—teaching techniques, teacher-made instructional materials, ways of providing extra support for struggling students. Even more challenging are the changes that matter most to us—the ones we believe will substantially improve student learning. These require an enormous commitment of energy and time, well beyond what schools provide via released time for inservice learning (Guskey, 2002). And then there's the fear factor. If we fail, the cost is high: Students will not learn as well as they would have otherwise. No wonder that we see change as "messy and trying," something that has us "running through cycles of trial and error, complaining about the difficulty of day-to-day coping, sacrificing other core activities, and feeling frustrated by unsuccessful attempts to make something work" (Adams, 2000, p. 9).

And yet, time and again, we make good-faith efforts to change, especially when the change is one for which we volunteer (Richardson, 1998). We don't change things like our approach to curriculum and instruction lightly or for our own sakes. Most of us enjoyed and succeeded in school—that's part of the reason we returned as teachers. But we are willing to change our strategies when we can see that school does not work for all students.

It is a good thing we are willing to make the enormous efforts sometimes needed for change to succeed. When it comes to the hard work of large scale change associated with reform movements, "If a teacher won't do it, it can't be done" (Hargreaves, Earl, Moore, & Manning, 2001, p. 120). Teachers are the conduit of reform, and reform efforts have their intended effect only when teachers are invested in them. As one teacher observed, if a teacher "doesn't believe the change will improve the teaching of children, reform is virtually impossible" (Foley, 1993, p. 12).

Despite a perception that teachers can be recalcitrant and resistant to change, there's plenty of evidence that we often are willing to face the challenge of change (e.g., Richardson & Placier, 2001). We do so because our psychic energy and reward comes from improving learning for our students. We do so in the hope that our efforts will contribute to making their lives better.

For teachers, change is inevitable. Dreading change does not have to be. There's an impressive body of literature, much of it from the field of management, designed to help people understand the change process so they can navigate it more easily. Understanding the principles and processes of change can help people in all sorts of complex organizations—in hospitals, airlines, and software companies, and also in schools (Fullan, 2001).

Unfortunately, the literature on educational change has been written primarily for administrators, not teachers. It overlooks the teacher's point of view, likely because the

---

[1] See the preface for details about the survey, which is reproduced as Appendix A.

impetus for change too often has come from people outside the classroom who determine that teachers must change what they are teaching, how they are teaching, or both. This top-down, mandated approach to change has not met with much success (Richardson & Placier, 2001) and too often has led to articles like the dismally titled "Why Teachers Resist Change (and What Principals Can Do About It)" (Richards, 2002).

With this book we hope to change things. *A Teacher's Guide to Change* was written to

- describe and analyze the changes teachers are likely to encounter across a career in education;
- help teachers understand the change process;
- lead teachers to examine and evaluate their typical responses to change, so they can alter them if they choose;
- demonstrate to teachers that they have the ability to do more than just survive change;
- teach them skills for navigating and managing change successfully; and
- encourage them to lead others in change.

Our purpose is to help teachers face the challenge of change with optimism and confidence, because we believe that will enable them to enjoy long and happy careers in education—and as a result, students will benefit. Huberman, Grounauer, & Marti (1993) found that teachers who have the highest level of professional satisfaction, sustained over many years, are those whose careers have been characterized by significant changes in grade levels, schools, and positions. Huberman interviewed a group of these teachers when they had between 30 and 40 years of experience, and he described them as "still energetic and committed, distinguish[ing] themselves from others by virtue of having a harmonious career at the outset and in their last phase" (Huberman et al., p. 250).

You will meet many such teachers in the pages of this book, and at times you will hear in their voices the trepidation and anxiety most of us experience when facing change. While some recount disappointing outcomes, most conclude that change has been a learning experience that helped them become better teachers. The stories of their experiences with change are the lifeblood of this book. In addition, you will find ways to make this book your own, by completing the Change Challenges we have developed, stimulated by the thoughts of participating teachers. We hope that this book will inspire you to reflect on the experiences you have already had and look ahead with new insights to the changes that await you.

CHAPTER 2

What Changes?

*Experiencing Change at
School and at Home*

In this chapter we'll hear from teachers about the professional and personal changes they have experienced and how these changes influenced their work in the classroom. Along the way, we'll consider the kinds of changes any of us might experience as our careers develop, how we might shape those changes, and what we can learn from them to strengthen our abilities as teachers.

I had been teaching fifth grade in the same school for 10 years when we had a major staff turnover. A retirement incentive scooped up many of the teachers with whom I had worked since I began teaching, the people who, without realizing it, taught me how to teach. I never hesitated to ask for their advice, and they never offered unless I asked. I hadn't known how much I depended on just seeing them every once in a while to keep my equilibrium. I missed them as colleagues and as friends.

The arrival of new colleagues changed my teaching life, though it took a while before I could see this change in a positive light. Their questions about some of our routines felt uncomfortable, and at first, I responded a bit defensively. But the questions made me take a second look at what I was doing. Most of the time, this renewed my enthusiasm for things that I had pretty much taken for granted. Before long, I saw that it really was curiosity and a desire to understand that prompted their questions.

I admit, with some chagrin now, that I was taken aback when they stopped asking questions and started making suggestions! I thought that should be *my* role! But these "newbies" have

(Continued)

(Continued)

different ideas about how teachers should work together. They just expect to collaborate. It's disarming, really. I've come to enjoy it. Now I am the one asking the questions.

The biggest change came because several of the new teachers were members of one of our state teaching organizations and encouraged me to get involved with it. By Thanksgiving, I realized that I had been on "automatic pilot" for a while with my teaching. Now I'm looking ahead with enthusiasm to a new phase in my professional life.

—Savannah, who has just volunteered to serve on the governmental relations committee of her state's elementary math teachers' association

CHANGES AT SCHOOL

The large scale reform efforts of the past three decades, launched with great fanfare and pursued at a relentless pace, serve to confirm at least one thing: Institutions only change when the people within them do (Adams, 2000). We can benefit from thinking critically about the authentic changes teachers experience and separating those from the hype. In this section, we will explore some of the changes teachers experience at school, including new administrators and colleagues, new teaching positions (sometimes in different schools), and the changes that accompany advanced education and professional recognition.

New Administration

The change most frequently noted in our research was a change in administration: 87% of the teachers in our survey said they had experienced a change in administration. They noted that administrative change brought other changes, especially new priorities and procedures, which had an impact on the daily lives of teachers.

Often teachers assessed these changes positively:

- "The hiring of a new director of special ed. has led to many new programs and increased student achievement."
- "With the new administrative team, I had the opportunity to have my opinions welcomed and my concerns responded to."

For some teachers, however, a change in administration had a negative impact:

- "A change at the top has meant a shift from a student-centered philosophy to an account-ability model, which has redefined the job of teaching here. The change has had a negative impact on me as a teacher."
- "Two new administrators fostered a negative climate and created a hostile work environment where people felt threatened and belittled."

Teachers also cited "frequent changes in administrative personnel" as harmful, leading to fragmentation of curriculum development efforts, inconsistent application of personnel policies, and sometimes "the feeling that I have to keep proving myself over and over." One teacher saw a silver lining to this cloud:

- "My district isn't big—a total of 2600 students in four schools. In my 23 years as a classroom teacher, we went through 17 principals and 23 superintendents, assistant superintendents, and business officers. The only thing that kept the district together was the faculty. We had to find our own way, and we became stronger as a result."

Change Challenge 2.1	Anticipating Administrative Change

What changes in administration can you expect in the next three years? Consider the administrators whose work can have a direct influence on your life as a teacher, for example, principal or assistant principal, director of special education or pupil personnel services, department chair, assistant superintendent for curriculum and instruction, or superintendent.

- Who is likely to leave, either to retire or to advance a career?
- What do you stand to lose when this person leaves?
- What could you gain?
- What qualities should your district look for in a replacement for this person?
- When the individual leaves, what can you do to have input into decisions about selecting a replacement? (For example, could you work with the teacher's union to develop a profile of the ideal candidate? Could you volunteer to serve on the search committee or take part in the interview process?)
- If you were trying to recruit a new administrator to your district, what one question would you ask of each potential candidate?
- Since new administrators are sometimes able to access resources or advance initiatives denied to previous administrators, what can you lobby for to strengthen your program?

New Teaching Positions

Preservice teachers talking about their futures sometimes say things like "I'm going to teach third grade" (or "AP Calculus" or "children with autism"). The teachers we surveyed might say, "Maybe . . . but probably not forever." Eighty-three percent of our teachers reported changing their grade level or content specialization, 74% reported a change in the student population they taught, and 63% said they experienced a change within their role at school (e.g., beginning to coteach or becoming a team leader).

I moved from being a classroom teacher to a literacy coach. I wanted to use my graduate training and to sharpen my skills and it was rewarding to help children who needed remediation in reading. But most of all I learned that I love being a classroom teacher and am most fulfilled by that. I am willing to make a move to a new district if that's what it takes for me to return to classroom teaching. If I have a choice, this time around I think I'd like to try working with older elementary children.

—LaTonya, who taught in inclusive classes at the K–3 level for five years before taking a position as a reading specialist

The changes teachers described as having a "major impact" included shifts in the following:

- *Who* is taught: Moving to a new grade level was seen as a significant change and often a welcome one. A special challenge develops when the new grade level introduces a significantly different age group, as when an art or music teacher who has been working at an elementary school moves to a high school.
- *What* is taught: A different content area can be problematic when it is outside the teacher's certification area or when it is a subject in which the teacher is certified but inexperienced.
- *With whom* we teach: Going from being a sole practitioner to a member of a team is a big change. Changes of membership within the team also call for readjustment.
- *The setting* for teaching: This change was most relevant for special education teachers and related service providers, who might shift among self-contained classrooms, resource programs, and inclusive classes.
- *Nonteaching responsibilities,* for example scheduling and budgeting: These might be part of new positions such as curriculum coordinator, department head, team leader, or grade level representative.

Day (2002) found that teachers who spontaneously sought some form of role shift every four or five years were more likely than other teachers to be happy in their work. The teachers in our study undoubtedly could relate to that: Those who described changes in position most often viewed them positively. They appreciated the chance to explore new curricula, get to know other colleagues, work with a different group of students, and in general grow professionally. Some described these changes as a way to become reenergized.

Becoming a coteacher after many years of flying solo was very beneficial for me, professionally and personally. I've been able to have contact with a greater range of students, which was a good challenge. I have learned so much from seeing how others do things, and I like trying out their new ways for myself. It was a good move.

—Guy, eighth-grade social studies teacher

What Changes?

Only 6% of the teachers responding to our question about changes with a negative impact mentioned a change in position, and all of their comments related to involuntary transfers. They described not feeling comfortable with a new content or age group and struggling to adjust in a new environment. Most of all, they were unhappy at not having a say in the reassignment.

> I was assigned to teach a new grade level without any prior discussion. I got along well with the other teachers in my grade, my children were making really good progress, and the parents seemed very happy with what was happening for their children. The reassignment came out of nowhere for myself and the other teacher. It made me second guess myself as an educator.
>
> —Vivianna, second-grade teacher reassigned to fifth grade

An interesting theme emerged from our surveys and interviews: Changes that are involuntary and initially unwelcome often work out well. Rose, an art teacher, expressed a sentiment shared by several others when she wrote, "My transfer from teaching high school level to elementary level was unwanted, but turned out to be a wonderful change for both my new students and me."

New Locations

About half (52%) of the teachers we surveyed reported moving to a new area or transferring to another school district nearby, with many of those reporting moves among public, private, and charter schools. While none of these moves was imposed by administration, not all were wholly voluntary. Some were the consequences of other events, like marriage or a spouse's relocation; some were the result of staff cutbacks.

> When my fiancée was transferred, I moved to Maryland. I had to update my certification to meet their requirements, which meant going back to grad school. I had to get used to a new set of curriculum frameworks and student assessments.
>
> —Darence, high school math teacher who moved from Florida to Maryland

Geneva Gay (2000) reminds us not to buy into the myth that "good teachers anywhere are good teachers everywhere" (p. 22). Moving to a new area often means adapting to a different culture, as was the case for a subset of 25 teachers invited to participate in a parallel study because they had made choices involving change—they moved from the northeast to teach in Hawaii. These young teachers (who made the move immediately following graduation from their teacher preparation programs) described the impact of the change as overwhelmingly positive. They valued the warmth and support of colleagues and administration and cherished the feeling of "ohana" (family) prevalent in their schools. Still, they often struggled to adapt their teaching strategies to meet the needs of children from a culture very different from their own, while also trying to adjust to unfamiliar customs and establish new networks of support. Teachers choosing to move from large urban schools to smaller suburban ones also reported adjustment challenges, such as learning how to respond to increased involvement and expectations of parents.

I chose to teach in a new charter school. There is an entirely different set of professional norms here, and I am still getting used to this way of working. The start-up has been hard, but I am glad to be working with a faculty and administration that share my value system.

—Nigel, now teaching in a small progressive 7–12 school
after 12 years in a large urban high school

Change Challenge 2.2	Considering New Options

As you complete the exercise below, think about how your talents and skills could be useful in a new setting.

	I'm confident I could be successful.	*I'd be willing to give this a try.*	*I'd need lots of convincing to try this.*	*No way.*
At a different grade level in my current school				
With a different content area				
With an unfamiliar group of students (students from other cultures or with disabilities)				
In a different school in my district				
In a different type of school (public, private, or charter; urban, suburban, or rural, etc.)				
In a different district within my state or region				
In a different part of the country or overseas				
In a new role (e.g., team leader, coteacher, remedial specialist, etc.)				

Which of these changes are you most likely to encounter in the next three years?

Go back and circle the one or two changes that you would be most interested in pursuing.

New Colleagues

The strongest statements we heard in the course of our research centered on relationships with colleagues. Time and again, teachers described the power of good colleagues to make school a place they wanted to come to every day as well as a place where they could find support and encouragement to grow in their effectiveness as teachers.

> The arrival of new colleagues has served to renew my enthusiasm and brought new commitment to my professional life.
>
> —Thom, a seventh- and eighth-grade social studies teacher, explaining his decision to suspend his plans for early retirement

The teachers in our study reported that working with beginning teachers fresh from teacher preparation programs exposed them to new ideas in curriculum and instruction. At the same time, establishing new relationships with seasoned colleagues helped teachers step up to a higher plane.

> When I moved from a remedial position to an inclusive class, I began collaborating with colleagues I had not known well before. I learned from their strengths and began to refine my teaching techniques. Working with people I respect and trust has made me a more thoughtful teacher.
>
> —Leo, now a team leader for Grade 5

These findings diverge from those of earlier education researchers (e.g., Little, 1990; Lortie, 2002; 1975), whose classic studies examining relationships among teachers led them to conclude that teaching is primarily a "private endeavor" (Little, p. 530) and that collaboration among teachers is not likely to be an avenue for teacher change. The teachers we studied repeatedly made the point that they learned to be better teachers from their interactions with their colleagues, saying "Working with other teachers constantly pushes me to grow" and "The two women I've taught with have been exceptional teachers and I have learned so much from them." We hope this is an indicator that an important change is underway in the teaching profession, one that Lieberman and Miller (1999) call the "transition from individualism to professional community" (p. 20).

Change Challenge 2.3   Learning From Each Other

Think of two teachers with teaching talents you admire that are different from yours. For each teacher, list admired skills, talents, or traits and complete the grid.

Teacher #1:		Teacher #2:

#1	*For each teacher, check off the things you'd be willing to do to learn from them:*	#2
	Talk casually during a shared lunch or prep period	
	Ask to borrow resources such as books or articles on the topic	
	Stop by after school to discuss a teaching problem related to the skill you admire	
	Ask for feedback on a sample of student work	
	Observe in the teacher's classroom	
	Ask the teacher to observe you	
	Suggest that the teacher make a presentation at your grade level or department meeting	
	Recommend that the teacher lead a workshop at the next Superintendent's Day conference	
	Volunteer to team teach	

Now turn the tables.

Name a teaching talent you have that others could use.

Circle the options above that you would agree to *if a colleague asked you for help.*

Professional Development

Good teachers never stop learning, and the teachers in our study identified advanced study as a professional change that had a major positive impact on their work. This may come as a surprise to critics of education for whom teacher education has been a handy scapegoat (see Karby, 2006, for discussion). But it is consistent with other research findings that professional development programs for teachers lead to increased competence on the job, greater professional satisfaction, and reduced risk of boredom and alienation (Guskey, 2002; Huberman, 1995; Richards, 2000).

Of the teachers we surveyed, 62% reported that they were pursuing or had completed a graduate degree. Several teachers noted that they began graduate work primarily because it was a state requirement for continued teacher certification or a district requirement for advancement. Only later did these teachers come to appreciate that their graduate studies helped them become better teachers.

- "When I moved to New York, I began graduate work, which I never would have pursued in Florida because it wasn't required. My grad work greatly influenced the way I teach now."

Others chose graduate programs that would create new career opportunities for them, often by leading to an additional teaching certificate. For example, an elementary teacher might become licensed as a reading specialist or a biology teacher might add a certificate in chemistry.

- "I earned a master's degree, which allowed me to get dual certification in elementary and special education. I am now more 'marketable.'"

Some teachers also noted that professional development workshops had been useful, particularly those focused on specialized approaches to curriculum and instruction, such as TEACCH and Reading Recovery. One teacher's statement was representative of many:

- "New training allowed me to provide better services to students."

There were, of course, costs associated with the benefits of pursuing advanced education. As one teacher wrote, "Because of the time I was spending on my graduate work and all of the late night commuting, my patience and the quality of my teaching I felt were not up to the standards I set for myself. Looking back I feel guilty, knowing I could have been different with those students."

Professional Recognition

We did not specifically ask the teachers we surveyed about awards and honors, but several volunteered that a change occurred when they achieved professional recognition for their work. The recognition came in many forms: selection as a member of a committee developing teacher certification tests; an invitation to teach part-time in a teacher-preparation program; election to the board of a regional professional organization for teachers; nomination by students to *Who's Who Among America's Teachers;* and selection as the district's Teacher of the Year. Several teachers who were awarded professional certification by the National Board of Professional Teaching Standards said that they regarded this achievement as a change with a significant impact.

There has been some attention to the uncomfortable consequences that may follow professional recognition. Quinn (1996) and Roettger (2006) report that a few teachers interpret one teacher's success as raising the bar for the rest. This was not mentioned by the teachers in our study. They spoke instead about gaining a new sense of themselves as professionals, sometimes accompanied by a greater sense of their obligation to help others develop as teachers.

> Being selected Teacher of the Year early in my career let me know my colleagues valued me. It also validated what I do and made me more sure of myself. Now I don't hesitate to offer my opinion when we are discussing problems with our classes. I also think that I am more willing to try new things now. The most important effect is I want to live up to the title I was given and prove myself worthy of it every day.
>
> —Diego, high school special education teacher in his fifth year of teaching

Change Challenge 2.4 Finding Ways to Grow

What professional development topics interest you?
(Some examples are literacy, numeracy, assessment, classroom management, collaboration, curriculum design, culturally responsive teaching, social-emotional development, service learning, etc.)

What are effective ways for you to access professional development?

- ❏ Traditional graduate course
- ❏ Noncredit courses
- ❏ Online courses
- ❏ Summer workshops
- ❏ Conference attendance
- ❏ Online discussion groups
- ❏ Teacher center mini courses
- ❏ Teacher book clubs
- ❏ One-to-one support from another teacher
- ❏ Reading relevant books or articles
- ❏ School-based inservice workshops

What forms of professional recognition would be meaningful for you?

- ❏ Letters from parents thanking you for your impact on their children
- ❏ Letters from former students explaining your influence on their lives
- ❏ Noteworthy achievement by your students
- ❏ Nomination by students for Teacher of the Year
- ❏ Nomination by colleagues for Teacher of the Year
- ❏ Being selected to represent your group on a schoolwide committee

---

- ❏ Being selected for membership on a districtwide committee
- ❏ Election to an office in your local teacher's union
- ❏ Election to an office in your state or regional professional organization
- ❏ Securing a mini-grant for a classroom project
- ❏ Being invited by a former professor to join a research project
- ❏ Obtaining an advanced degree or certification
- ❏ Achieving certification by the National Board of Professional Teaching Standards (NBPTS)

Others: _____

What are you doing currently that could lead to this recognition?_____

_____

_____

What else could you do if you decided that you wanted to earn professional recognition?

_____

_____

When one teacher told us about her most challenging year in teaching, she described the year that saw the arrival of a new principal, who reassigned her to a different grade level and a new teaching team, just as she was embarking on the research project required for her master's degree. "That was nothing," she said. "It was learning that I was unexpectedly pregnant with our third child that just about did me in." In the next section of this chapter, we'll take a look at how changes in teachers' personal lives affect their professional lives.

CHANGES IN LIFE AT HOME

For many of us, teaching is much more than a job. It is a career, a vocation, even a calling. Teaching is not only what we do, it helps define who we are (e.g., Huberman, Grounauer, & Marti, 1993). So it is understandable that efforts to bring about educational change fail when they neglect "the teacher as a person, abstracting the teacher's skills from the teacher's self, the technical aspects of the teacher's work from the commitments embedded in the teacher's life" (Hargreaves, quoted in Huberman et al., p. viii).

These commitments in our personal lives can serve to enrich our professional lives. As we mature through our personal relationships, we strengthen the human relations skills so necessary for us to be effective as teachers. Our interests outside of school provide an important balance to our work lives, allowing us to "step back and relativize the problems that come up in the classroom" (Huberman et al., p. 253). It follows then that the *changes* we experience in our personal lives will reverberate in our classrooms.

While we are experiencing the work-life changes described in the first half of this chapter, we are simultaneously coping with changes at home. Some of those changes are huge and require enormous amounts of time and energy. While they were teaching, 58% of the teachers in our study got married, 46% had a major change in family responsibilities, 60% added a new child to their family, and 61% lost a loved one. A major change in economic circumstances was reported by 37%, and 15% divorced. Inevitably, these developments in teachers' personal lives have an impact on their performance at work. *An important theme throughout teachers' comments was that as a result of managing life changes, including those that are painful, teachers have more to offer to their students and are more effective in the classroom.* As one teacher said, "I have found over the years that the strength that comes from overcoming personal issues transfers to the strengths one develops as a teacher. I am a much stronger and tougher teacher than I was 10 years ago, but also a more empathetic and careful teacher."

Illness

About a quarter of the teachers we surveyed reported that they (or members of their households) had experienced a major illness at some point during their careers. While these illnesses must have caused the teachers to be absent from work and perhaps distracted while at work, those were not the themes they emphasized in the comments they wrote on the survey. When discussing the impact of illness, they noted unexpected benefits. For some, illness led to a change in how they viewed and interacted with students:

> • "I had cancer. The positive impact was it made me more compassionate toward my students. I realized more viscerally that many of them experienced situations that were difficult and they were so young and without the experience to cope well."
> • "I try to offer advice about dealing with major life changes using my experiences with cancer as an example."

For others, illness brought about reflection and a recommitment to teaching:

> • "After a major illness, I updated my certification and made a move to special education because I thought I could have a greater impact on the lives of these students."
> • "Dealing with cancer as a young adult made me appreciate my time with teaching. It made me see the immediate importance of my life and my responsibilities as a teacher of young children."

Loss

The death of a loved one is, of course, the hardest change most of us will encounter. We deeply appreciate that teachers were willing to share their reflections on the changes they experienced as a result of losing a family member.

Some teachers did not elaborate much on the impact of their loss beyond indicating that they just did what they could to make it through another day:

> • "The death of my parents—both during the school year—had me going through the motions for a time."
> • "The illness and death of my husband made it difficult to maintain my focus on work over the years. But for the most part, I had a lot of support from family, friends, and colleagues at school, so I was able to keep going."

What Changes?

A few mentioned that the work of teaching, and the support of colleagues, helped them push through.

- "I have great pride in my work and enjoy my students, so it has helped me deal with personal changes in life such as the illness and death of my mother, to whom I was very close. It has given me great consolation in dealing with the death of a loved one, because life goes on when you are dealing with young people on a daily basis."
- "Being at school, and especially coaching after school, helped after I lost my wife. The other coaches and even the kids understood that I needed the distraction."

Some used their experiences with the death of a family member to help students facing similar losses.

- "My mother died when I was a child, and I have used what I learned through my grief in working with four different students who have lost parents. . . . I have enough experience to relate to these kids and to reach out to those who are experiencing such profound losses."
- "I can help students who lose a parent since I had to deal with my own children and their loss of a father."

For some teachers, the death of a loved one brought into sharper focus their purpose as teachers.

- "The losses of my father and a dear friend have helped me to keep many of the stresses associated with state testing and daily clerical responsibilities in perspective. It has helped me remember to take time to enjoy the students and the learning process in spite of the external stresses."
- "I have learned we are all replaceable, life will go on, and I need to do what's best for kids, no matter what. I push harder now to get kids what they need."

Change Challenge 2.5	Questions for Reflection

1. In what ways have painful experiences helped you to develop qualities that you value in yourself today?

2. In what ways have those qualities helped you to become a better teacher?

(Continued)

(Continued)

3. How have you been able to assist other teachers as a result of these personal experiences?

Changes in Relationships and Responsibilities

Teachers juggle their responsibilities to students and colleagues at the same time as they are evolving in their roles as sons and daughters, husbands and wives, friends and lovers. When new family responsibilities are added, teachers can feel overwhelmed.

> A big change occurred this year when my father moved in with us. Now I have to use my prep periods at school to manage his care—call for doctor's appointments, check on insurance payments, that sort of thing. Instead of talking with the aide at lunch about what we're doing in the afternoon, I call to check on my father and break up his day a little. Two minutes after the busses leave, I'm gone, too, because I have a million errands I didn't have before. I haven't had to take any sick days yet, but neither have I been fully present, mentally or physically.
>
> —Ruth, fourth-grade inclusive class teacher

Problems in our personal lives also can take an emotional toll that interferes with our ability to concentrate at school.

- "A serious personal situation with my own teenaged child was very disruptive to my ability to perform my job. I was constantly preoccupied. I would fill up with tears without warning."
- "I was in a personal relationship that ended badly and was quite devastating."
- "Being in debt is stressful. I am anxious and unfocused at work."

But with time, we develop strategies that allow us to manage our new responsibilities. We then bring to our classrooms an increased capacity for dealing with life's challenges.

- "When I became the primary caregiver to my parents, my skills in multitasking were particularly honed."
- "I feel my husband's illness forced me to learn how to manage my time better and not worry about little things."
- "I used the experience of bouncing back after my divorce to remember that all things will eventually work themselves out."

What Changes?

Parenting

When we asked teachers open-ended questions about the changes in their personal lives that had a major impact on their professional lives, they most often talked about becoming parents. There were scores of variations on one teacher's simple statement:

"I became a more effective teacher when I became a parent."

Very few comments noted drawbacks to teachers becoming parents; those that did were of a pragmatic nature, such as, "Now that I have my own children, I obviously have less time to devote to teaching," and "I used to think nothing of buying books and supplies for my classroom, but now that I have a family, I can't do that anymore." Most comments, instead, called attention to the benefits teachers gain from their experiences as parents.

Some changes occur simply because new parents develop skills they didn't need before:

> I used to be very laid back. Back then I would have said I was spontaneous and flexible. Now I see it differently, and maybe it's more honest to say I was lax or at least too easygoing. When my daughter was born, everything changed. I have to be super organized and on target to get her through the whole big morning routine and into the car by 7:30 each morning, and then be ready to leave school on time so I can do it in reverse at 3:30. It has changed me at work. I accomplish a lot more than I did before.
>
> —Dayna, science teacher for Grades 7 and 8 and mother of a three-year-old

Some teachers noted that parenting helped them see school from a new perspective:

- "Having my own children, watching their reactions to various teachers and types of school work and experiences helps me to remember that I am working with someone else's daughters and sons."

Others observed that parenthood gives teachers greater understanding of parents' concerns and more skill in working with families:

- "I became a parent of four, which gave me a new perspective on parenting and on home-school partnerships. It made me a better teacher and also made me more empathetic to parents."
- "Being a working mother, I have learned that family time is as important as school time. Children should not be spending countless hours at home doing homework. Therefore, I only send home work that is meaningful and productive and on occasion will get family members involved."

The most frequent observation from teachers in our study, however, was that once they become parents, teachers view children differently. Their comments echo Michael Huberman, whose in-depth study of 160 secondary school teachers over five years led him to conclude, "The relationship with one's own children and their school experiences seems to influence directly the relationship between the teacher and the students" (Huberman et al., 1993, p. 253). The teachers in our study reported that having sons and daughters of their own led them to have a deeper appreciation for individual differences, to be more patient, and to respond to students with empathy and compassion more readily.

- "When I became a mother I became more patient and understanding with my students."
- "Through my own children I have learned to be more aware, open-minded, and accepting of individual differences in personality, learning style, strengths, and weaknesses."
- "My empathy with and compassion for my students increased."

Some comments seemed to offer an explanation for why parenthood leads to changes in how teachers view students:

- "When I had my first, and only, child, my teaching style changed. I then began to approach my students with an idea in mind, 'How would I want a teacher to work with my child, talk with my child, help my child, and model for my child?'"
- "Having my own child... made me more patient with students because I try to think of how I would want my own child treated in school."

It's important to note that teachers who are parents have no monopoly on the traits and skills described above. Certainly teachers who are *not* parents are also kind, patient, empathetic, and able to see things from a parent's point of view. They simply develop these traits by other means.

Change Challenge 2.6 | Questions for Reflection

1. As you add new responsibilities in your personal life (for example, as a spouse, parent, caregiver, in-law, companion, or friend) what *skills* are you developing that can help you as a teacher?

2. What new *perspectives* can you gain that will enhance your understanding of students?

3. As a result of new relationships, what *personal qualities* can you develop that strengthen your ability to fulfill your aspirations as a teacher?

CONNECTING OUR PROFESSIONAL AND PERSONAL CHANGES TO THE CHANGE THAT MATTERS MOST

So what? What's so important about understanding what happens when we begin to work with new administrators or move to a new grade level, or when we experience a shift in our personal lives?

Actually, it's only important to the extent that it influences student learning. The professional changes described in this chapter are significant only when they influence curriculum and instruction and give us more powerful tools to help children develop the knowledge and skills that we as a society deem important (Brown & Moffett, 1999; Fullan, 2001; Hargreaves, Earl, Moore, & Manning, 2001). When the teachers in our study described the practical effects of the changes they experienced at school, they focused on curriculum and instruction:

Changes in Administration

- "A new administration brought in a curriculum development program that has helped me and my students."

Changes in Teaching Position

- "Becoming an inclusion teacher helped me to better meet the needs of all students and accommodate all needs."

New Colleagues

- "In recent years we have hired many young and creative teachers. I have been able to adopt and adapt many of their innovations for use in my classroom."

Professional Development

- "Taking classes toward my master's changed my beliefs and teaching style for the better."

Professional Recognition

- "National board certification allowed me to evaluate and improve my teaching."

Similarly, changes in our lives at home matter because they are likely to have an effect on the personal resources that we bring to our work with students, for example, by broadening our perspective or deepening our understanding:

- "My becoming a parent made me a much more effective teacher. I ceased being a 'child-raising expert' and became much more aware of the need for patience, compassion, and a sense of humor when dealing with other people's children."
- "My son's ADHD has helped me to be more sensitive to the needs of students who struggle with this condition in school."
- "The death of a brother has made me more aware of the things students are dealing with and more open to sharing feelings with students."

Looking Ahead

For better or for worse, teachers' personal and professional lives intersect. As one teacher wrote on our survey, "Everything that we experience in life is, in some way, brought into the classroom." When we can anticipate the changes we are likely to encounter across a career in teaching, we are in a better position to navigate those changes and use them to become more effective teachers.

In the next chapter we'll explore how change affects us by considering some dimensions of change. What are the differences between change that is voluntary rather than mandated, or top-down instead of bottom-up, or incremental rather than fundamental? How do those differences influence our response to change?

CHAPTER 3

Defining the Dynamics of Change for Teachers

Consider three teachers, all faced with the same task: replacing a car.

- Elena can't wait to get rid of her minivan. With her youngest son now a licensed driver safely ensconced in his grandmother's old Volvo, her days of carting half the hockey team and mountains of sports equipment are over. This time, she's looking for a car that will suit her needs and reflect her style. She's even thinking of going to the car dealerships without her husband.
- Marcy was rear-ended as she was driving home from her second job teaching a GED prep class. She teaches two nights a week because the child support payments that seemed fair 10 years ago are woefully inadequate now that her three daughters are teens. She didn't have collision insurance on the 10-year-old car and she has no money to replace it. She is angry, resentful, and overwhelmingly anxious.
- Justin's beloved Miata, his pride and joy since he was 19, needs major repairs. He knows it doesn't make sense to fix it; the car is utterly impractical for a man with a wife and six-month-old son. He's been saving for a family car, and with the money he'll get from selling the Mazda, he'll be able to buy a good used car without taking out a loan. He has no problem moving ahead with the adult responsibilities he has willingly taken on. The problem is in saying good-bye to what his Miata represents and in trying to picture himself in a four-door sedan.

Our experiences with change at school can be as varied and colored by emotion as the decisions Elena, Marcy, and Justin must make about their cars. Some changes we seek out, plan for carefully, and anticipate with relish. Sometimes change blindsides us, or is imposed, and leaves us stunned, angry, or hurt. Sometimes we know we need to make a change, and we want to do so, but we experience paralysis all the same. The teachers in our study described all of these responses and more. In Chapter 2, we described the kinds of change teachers experience; in Chapter 3, we will explore some dimensions of change that may influence our responses to it.

VOLUNTARY OR MANDATED

As noted in the last chapter, researchers have established that teachers often *choose* to make changes (e.g., Guskey, 2002; Richardson & Placier, 2001). When we asked teachers how often the major changes in their professional lives were made voluntarily, only 18% said "seldom or never"; 56% said the major changes they experienced as teachers were voluntary "about half of the time," and 27% said they were voluntary "all or most of the time" (see Figure 3.1).

Throughout this book, you will read about the many voluntary changes teachers described to us in surveys and interviews. The range of undertakings is impressive, and in the teachers' comments, their pride and enthusiasm sparkle. Because voluntary change is described later, we'll concentrate on mandated change in this section. Before we do, we want to note that despite the optimism with which we undertake voluntary change, it sometimes doesn't work out as well as we hope, for ourselves or our students.

Figure 3.1 How often have the major changes in your life as a teacher been voluntary?

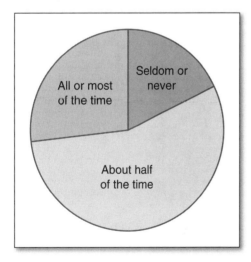

A few teachers we interviewed reported that they chose to move to new schools or into new administrative positions, but eventually returned to their original positions, finding that the new roles and responsibilities were not the good fit they had anticipated. Richardson (1998) also notes that "voluntary change . . . does not necessarily lead to exemplary teaching" as when a teacher enthusiastically embarks on a new approach to teaching and, because she has invested so much time and energy, keeps at it despite evidence that it is not working well.

Most of the time, however, teachers are pleased with the outcomes of voluntary change. The same cannot be said for mandated change. Mandated change can take many forms: new procedures for communicating with parents, additional documentation for disciplinary referrals, or mandatory participation in professional development activities. But the mandated change that prompted some of the strongest sentiments expressed by teachers during our study centered on involuntary transfer to a new grade level or school. The teachers who shared their stories with us saw involuntary transfers as unwarranted, sometimes as punitive, and almost always as burdensome.

I was pretty active in the union—I was a building rep, was on the contract negotiations team, that kind of thing. I was always one to speak up for individual rights—not just for teachers but also student rights, which were threatened by the mindless "zero tolerance" policies the new administration pushed into the behavior code. Last June, one year before my planned retirement, I was transferred from the middle school where I had taught sixth grade for 23 years and assigned to teach second grade at the primary school. This was a mean-spirited, counterproductive, and transparent attempt on the part of administration to muzzle me.

I'm sorry to say, they have been pretty successful. It is all I can do to keep up with a new curriculum and unfamiliar tests. I know what effective teaching is, and I know I'm missing the mark most of the time, despite the fact that I now spend more time preparing for classes than I have in years. Also, the faculty at this school is younger, mostly untenured, and too worried about job security to speak up for themselves or their students. What little power they could have, they refuse to take.

It has left a bitter taste in my mouth.

—Sally, veteran teacher with 30 years' experience, most in a single school district

Mandated change at school is especially stressful when teachers are coping with change at home:

Upon my return to work after the birth of my twins, my principal unnecessarily decided to change my grade level. He moved another unwilling teacher into my position. The change caused a rift within the building between teachers and caused parent complaints. The new grade level required many inservice training sessions during the school year that necessitated travel of more than an hour into treacherous snow country during the winter. That also meant that I was absent from the classroom and substitutes taught my class often. When I needed to take a sick day to care for my twins or my own health, it added to the amount of time I was away from the classroom. I actually did not attend the funeral of a close relative in order to minimize the time away from my class. If I had it to do over, I would not again choose to miss a funeral.

—Shanna, veteran teacher with eight years' experience, all in the same school

Fortunately, not all involuntary transfers have such dire consequences.

I now realize my involuntary transfer was a good thing. I was too comfortable in my last position. I knew the job like the back of my hand and I was very bored. I often "phoned it in." I needed a change to make my work life interesting and challenging, but I didn't know this until change was thrust upon me.

—Rosa, who was reassigned from a self-contained special education class at the primary level to a middle school resource room

In Chapter 4, we will introduce you to another involuntarily reassigned teacher, who went "kicking and screaming" from an elementary school to a high school and ended up loving her new position. It is important to keep in mind that changes that are involuntary and distinctly unwelcome at first can work out well.

Change Challenge 3.1	Examining Voluntary and Mandated Change

Think about a *voluntary change* you made in your personal or professional life.

In what ways did that change turn out to be less than you hoped for?

What did you do to adjust?

Now think about a *mandated change*.

In what ways did it work out better than you expected?

How do you explain the unexpected outcome?

As you consider these two experiences, what can you learn about how you respond to change?

TOP-DOWN OR BOTTOM-UP

"Governors, legislators, state superintendents of education . . . in my classroom?" Well, yes, in a way, and they've been there for years. Most of the change efforts in education represent attempts by those in the upper echelons of power to influence what happens in classrooms (Cuban, 1988). Curriculum frameworks developed at the state level, tied to tests required by federal legislation; policies for promotion and retention based on those test scores; course offerings shaped by graduation requirements set at the state capitol—all of these are examples of top-down changes that impact teachers.

Richardson and Placier (2001) describe top-down change as beginning with researchers and policy makers, then being filtered through school administrators, before finally being passed on to teachers. They contrast this with bottom-up change, which they describe as coming from "the autonomy, growth and problem-solving ability of people who make up the system (i.e. the teachers)" (p. 906). Site-based management, shared decision making, and decentralization are examples of structures that promote bottom-up change.

Teachers are very clear about the damage that can result from top-down change:

> When asked if teachers had input into the decision to restructure [and thereby to embark on block scheduling and interdisciplinary team teaching], Lew said, "Not at all, not at all, and you will find that to be the case in most of the things that are passed down to us, and that is what keeps a lot of the dissension, and that is what keeps a lot of the indifference, to tell you the truth." (Meister & Nolan, 2001, p. 613)

Many teachers in our study share the frustration that is audible in Lew's comment. A focus for their discontent was a hot-button issue at the time of the study: the requirements for statewide testing that were part of the No Child Left Behind legislation. Asked to identify changes with a major negative impact, teachers wrote the following:

- "The NCLB legislation. I think that some special ed. students are in classes and taking tests that have no relevance to their lives."
- "Over the years I loved opportunities for creativity—web quests, plays, field trips, etc. I enjoyed going to conferences to refresh and improve my practice. As the politics of state testing began to grab hold . . . the focus has become drilling and cramming even more information into students' brains in less time."
- "On the middle school level, for many years there was more flexibility to do the kinds of lessons that were appropriate for children of that age; things that made learning fun, interesting, and successful for both student and teacher. With the introduction of state testing, many facets of my program had to be shortened or dropped. Teaching to the test has been the result of the state standards, making the creative part of the job and the rewards that much less apparent."

These teachers would not be surprised to learn that there is not much research support for the effectiveness of top-down efforts (e.g., Cuban, 2004; Hall & Hord, 2001). Hargreaves, Earl, Moore, and Manning (2001) vividly describe the problem: "A common administrative and legislative delusion and conceit is that reform can be imposed, even forced, on teachers without any regard for their values or inclusion of their voices. Historically, this pattern of forced implementation has enjoyed little or no success" (p. 128).

The observations of Fullan (1994) are consistent with Hargreaves et al.: Top-down strategies that don't engender outright rebellion typically result in merely surface compliance.

Their dismal record notwithstanding, top-down efforts to impose change continue to be the dominant mode (Hall & Hord, 2001). Why? For one reason, while top-down change is far from ideal, it can work. Meister and Nolan (2001) studied five teachers who were required to implement a major change they had no say in. The teachers were angry and hurt that they and their colleagues had been excluded from the discussions that led to the decision to restructure their school, but

> despite intense feelings of doubt and uncertainty, these five teachers engaged in almost heroic efforts to make things succeed so their students would benefit. Their commitment to student welfare in the face of the emotional turmoil they experienced throughout the change effort was remarkable. (p. 612)

Another reason for the persistence of top-down approaches is that bottom-up efforts tend not to flourish for long, instead losing steam before drifting away completely (Fullan, 1994). Hall and Hord (2001) suggest this happens because those at the top retain for themselves decision-making authority on the issues that matter most and do not allocate sufficient resources to support the change efforts of the bottom. Richardson and Placier (2001) also note that bottom-up approaches, which tend to emerge where there is a climate of teacher autonomy and individualism, carry a risk of harm to students. Changes in curriculum and instruction may be implemented unevenly and in idiosyncratic ways that can result in "a dramatic lack of coherence" (p. 938) in the school experiences of individual students as they encounter different teachers from one year to the next.

No wonder educational change expert Michael Fullan concludes that "neither top-down nor bottom-up strategies are effective" (Fullan, 1994, p. 1). So where's the hope for meaningful change? Fullan maintains that it lies in using both approaches simultaneously, with those at the top providing direction, insuring adequate resources, and monitoring progress, while those at the bottom use their creativity to respond to individual circumstances and modify the change effort as needed. That seems to be the approach some teachers are taking in response to the top-down imposition of testing requirements.

A couple of years back our special ed. department developed a reading program that was very different from what was used in general ed.—more of a direct instruction approach, with more emphasis on phonics. However, when NCLB came in, we were told that all students had to take the same standards-based grade level assessments. The assessments matched the regular ed. program but not the special ed. The implication from our principal was that we should go back to using what we already knew did not work for our kids.

Some of us were not willing to just abandon all of the work we had done. We worked to find a way to bridge the gap. We did it by creating benchmark assessments based on the state tests and finding alternate reading texts to shore up our weak areas. We concentrated on the parts of the state test that were most appropriate for our students, like vocabulary and comprehension, and didn't worry too much about the more esoteric parts, like the literary terms. It was a stressful and time-consuming undertaking. It negatively impacted me at the time, but it positively helped student achievement. Our kids are now exposed to more content than they had been in the past, and I guess that is one of the points of NCLB.

—Jude, teacher in a self-contained special education class for Grades 4, 5, and 6

Change Challenge 3.2	Questions for Reflection

- If you are struggling with a top-down change, what could you and your colleagues do to mount a bottom-up response that would result in better outcomes all around?

- Identify one or two educational issues important enough to you that you would be willing to join a teacher-led campaign to address them.

- How can you use your voice to influence the policy makers at the top who decide on important educational issues?

INCREMENTAL OR FUNDAMENTAL

Several years ago I was part of a team that started a new, progressive high school in New York City. I was not prepared for how much work the change would be. Almost nothing from my previous job could be used in the new school, even though I was teaching high school English in both places. There wasn't a single unit—maybe not even a single lesson—that I could use without adapting it and modifying it somehow.

Partly this was because the new school was much more diverse. We designed it as a community school and one of our goals was to eliminate ability tracking. My classes were mixed ability levels, mixed cultures, mixed socioeconomic levels, some students who spoke very little English, some who could barely read—you name it. It was a challenge. I don't know how I would have managed if I hadn't already been an experienced teacher. At least I had a basic toolkit I could use as I was trying to figure out how to teach all these different kids.

I was so busy keeping up with planning lessons and grading papers that I kind of lost sight for a while of the reasons we started the school. We had endless faculty meetings where we talked about things like vision and mission, but I was working so hard to keep my head above water I didn't

(Continued)

(Continued)

really tune in. Somewhere during the second year, when I had a minute to catch my breath, I noticed that we actually were doing what we set out to do—we were becoming the community of learners we had aspired to be. Most of us had been able to ditch the "chalk and talk, sage on the stage" model we had grown up with. We were learning right alongside the students, trying to follow their lead and go with their interests. Parents and other family members were there all the time, as both volunteers and visitors. We used the whole city as our learning lab. We had kids out in the community every day, long before "service learning" became a buzzword.

The school was small, and we had the same students several years in a row, so we got to know them well. That may have been the biggest change. I entered their lives, and they entered mine, to a degree I have not experienced since. It expanded my concept of what it means to be a teacher.

—Ricardo, a pioneer in the alternative schools movement of the 1980s

Ricardo's moving account illustrates both incremental and fundamental change (Cuban, 1992, 2007; Waks, 2007). Incremental change, also called first-order change, refers to the things we do to make improvements to existing practices, without altering structural issues like how the school is organized or how teachers perform their roles. When Ricardo modifies a lesson plan he used in his previous school to make it better suited to his current classes, he is engaged in incremental change. The teachers in our study reported dozens and dozens of instances of incremental change. Some of those were in their own classrooms, such as the following:

- Recruiting senior citizens as classroom volunteers or foster grandparents
- Securing a grant to build a hothouse to use in science instruction
- Adopting new approaches to behavior management
- Developing and teaching a new honors curriculum
- Infusing technology into instruction

At other times teachers made incremental changes that were felt in the wider school community, such as the following:

- Developing a schoolwide disabilities awareness program
- Revising the elementary science curriculum to make it inquiry based
- Setting up a cross-age after-school tutoring program
- Establishing cocurricular clubs (school newspaper, drama club, math team)
- Bringing in a peer mediation program

In contrast, fundamental change (also called second-order change) takes place when there is a sense that the current structures are not working and need to be transformed. The goals of the organization are changed, and the ways people work within the organization are radically altered. As an example of fundamental change, Cuban (1988) cites the move from the one-room schoolhouse, with children of all ages taught by an unsupervised teacher, to schools organized by grade levels, with a formal curriculum taught by teachers who are supervised by principals. The progressive urban school Ricardo describes—which was governed by the faculty, housed various social agencies, and served as a multi-purpose community center—represents a fundamental change from traditional high schools. Ricardo's conclusion that teaching there left him with an expanded concept of what it means to be a teacher also suggests that the experience represented a fundamental change.

In Cuban's view, most educational change has been incremental and has served to maintain the existing practices of schooling. Though fundamental changes have been tried—such as open classrooms, mastery learning, nongraded schools, individualized instruction, and open-space architecture—they "were installed and dismantled, barely denting existing practice" (Cuban, 1988, p. 230). This may be because fundamental change is much more complex and proceeds more slowly, relying as it does on changes in how teachers interact with their students and each other (Stiegelbauer, 1994).

There was little mention of fundamental change in the surveys and interviews we conducted, but two topics that came up regularly *could* lead to fundamental change: educational technology and inclusive education. The potential for technology, and especially distance education, to transform the process of schooling is easy to see. Less obvious but just as powerful is the potential for inclusive education to alter our understanding of the purposes of schooling, for students with and without disabilities, as well as to reshape the roles and responsibilities of teachers (e.g., Burstein, Sears, Wilcoxen, Cabello, & Spagna, 2004). When the teachers we surveyed brought up changes related to technology and to inclusive education, however, they described incremental change:

- "The advent of the use of computers in schools . . . had major positive impacts on my ability to diversify instruction and enjoy teaching."
- "Moving to an inclusive setting from a self-contained class (led to) collaborating with colleagues, delivering better instruction and assessments, refining teaching techniques, and learning from others' strengths."

Proponents of educational technology and inclusive education may find hope in this. Changes that endure are a combination of incremental and fundamental change, with incremental change predominating (Cuban, 1988). Moreover, teachers develop the new beliefs and attitudes that are necessary for fundamental change only after they have seen—through incremental change—that new programs result in improvements in student learning (Guskey, 2002).

Change Challenge 3.3 Analyzing Changes in Your Professional Life

Think back to the changes you have experienced as a teacher:

A different school? A new principal or department head? Change in grade level or subject? A new role as a teacher-leader or coteacher? Revisions in curriculum standards or instructional strategies? Alterations in classroom organization or behavior management? Old colleagues leaving, new ones arriving? New ways of working with other teachers and paraprofessionals? Enhanced skills as a result of professional development courses or graduate work? Professional recognition leading to a stronger sense of yourself as a teacher?

(Continued)

(Continued)

Using your experiences with change, complete the table below. In the process, you will begin to analyze the changes you have encountered in your professional life.

Think of a Change That...	Name the Change	Voluntary or Mandatory?	Top-down or Bottom-up?	Incremental or Fundamental?
you welcomed and that worked out well				
was positive, though you were initially wary				
worked out well but was difficult to manage				
was easy to manage but had little value				
was not worth the effort it took to manage it				
had a negative impact				

Look over your responses. Are patterns evident that can help you understand how different kinds of change affect you as a teacher?

Looking Ahead

In Part I of *A Teacher's Guide to Change,* we considered the essential and pervasive nature of change in education, surveyed the different kinds of change teachers experience, and explored key characteristics of change. With this background knowledge, we are ready to take a closer look at how we manage the change process in both our personal and professional lives. In Part II, we'll look at what we can expect to think, feel, and do as the change process unfolds.

PART II

Understanding the Change Process

In Part I of *A Teacher's Guide to Change*, we looked at the wide array of personal and professional changes a teacher might experience across a career in education. In Part II, we focus more narrowly, taking a closer look at all that happens to us as we make a change. In Chapter 4, we examine the way people typically respond when they first encounter a change, paying special attention to why teachers may resist change. In Chapter 5, we explore two different ways of describing the phases of the change process.

CHAPTER 4

First Encounters
With Change

The prospect of change elicits a range of responses from us, consistent with our individual differences. But we can detect commonalities in our responses, too, if we look closely. In this chapter, we will explore ways teachers respond to innovation and the reasons we sometimes resist change.

RESPONDING TO INNOVATION

I've never wanted to be the first one to jump into a swimming pool. I'm happy to let others test the waters, and then wade in once I can see that everything's fine.

—Cristina, speech therapist, 26 years' experience

I love new gadgets, and can't wait to get my hands on the next one. Whenever a new "tech toy" comes into our building—like the Smartboard—I'm the first one to try it out.

—Sevim, primary and intermediate teacher, 31 years' experience

Cristina and Sevim have lots in common. Both women are over 50, mothers of grown sons, and lifelong teachers who have belonged to the same book club for 12 years. They share many beliefs and values, but they couldn't be more different in how they approach new experiences. That wouldn't surprise Everett Rogers a bit.

For over 40 years, Rogers (1995) has studied people who are faced with implementing a change, for example, doctors integrating the use of new medications into their medical practices and farmers using new hybrid crops. He has found that, rich or poor, educated or illiterate, rural or urban, in countries all over the world, *individuals differ in their readiness to adopt a change, and these differences follow a predictable pattern.*

Innovations in Educational Practices

Rogers's work on innovation is relevant to our exploration of teachers and change because so many of the changes teachers must make involve adopting innovations. Practices that today are taken for granted as essential elements in a teacher's repertoire of skills were innovations to an earlier generation of teachers. Consider these innovations—past and present—mentioned by the teachers in our study:

- Alternative assessments for students with significant cognitive deficits
- Balanced literacy
- Block scheduling
- Blogs, wikis, podcasts, and other student- and teacher-generated content shared electronically
- Classroom Web sites maintained by the teacher
- Communication boards for students with significant disabilities
- Community–based instruction
- Concept mapping
- Constructivist approaches to curriculum design and lesson planning
- Cooperative learning
- Coteaching and team teaching
- Curriculum differentiation
- Curriculum mapping
- Curriculum-based assessment
- Integrated units
- Interdisciplinary teaching
- Looping
- Multiage classrooms
- Online individualized education program (IEP) preparation
- Peer coaching
- Peer conferencing
- Peer mediation
- Performance assessment
- Portfolio assessment
- Reading Recovery
- Reciprocal teaching
- Service learning
- Student-centered rather than teacher-directed modes of instruction
- Student-led parent-teacher conferences and IEP meetings
- Technology-enhanced instructional strategies, such as WebQuests and computer simulations
- Universal Design for Learning

Looking over this list, it is hard to imagine how teachers could survive in education if we were unwilling to explore innovations. Rogers uses the term *innovativeness* to describe an individual's openness to making a change in behavior.

Categorizing Responsiveness to Innovation

Rogers regards innovativeness as a trait that is distributed in humans in a pattern that follows the normal curve, similar to height, weight, or intelligence. (For example, a few of us are quite short, a few are unusually tall, and most of us cluster around the middle, with "average" representing a fairly broad range.) Rogers says people generally fall into one of five categories of innovativeness, or openness to adopting a change. (See Figure 4.1.)

Innovators are, to use Rogers's term, *venturesome.* They enjoy trying out new ways of doing things and are excited by the possibilities inherent in innovations, even risky ones. Innovators are perceived by others as daring and sometimes as rash or naïve. They are able to tolerate uncertainty and to deal with disappointment and setbacks when the innovation falls short of its promise. When Gerri-Anne, a general education teacher and Tim, a special education teacher, chose to combine their programs to create an inclusive classroom 30 years ago, in the absence of administrative prompting and without any models to follow, they were behaving like innovators. Rogers expects only 2 to 3% of the population to be described as innovators; the faculty in your school probably includes only a few innovators, and if your school is small, may not include any.

There are sure to be some *early adopters* among your faculty though; about 13 to 14% of the population proves to be early adopters. Rogers describes this group as *respected* since they are known for making judicious decisions about change, and their colleagues often look to them for information and advice about new developments. Early adopters experience the anxiety about change that most of us feel, but they deal with it by adopting a new practice thoughtfully, evaluating it, and conveying the information to their peers. As a result, early adopters are regarded as opinion leaders and often serve as role models for others who are contemplating the change. People who volunteer to pilot a new curriculum package or to serve on the school's first shared decision-making committee could be accurately described as early adopters.

The *early majority* is one of the two large groups, constituting about 34% of the population. Rogers calls this group *deliberate.* They think carefully, often for a long time, before proceeding to adopt an innovation. They are willing to make a change, but are cautious in doing so. Most early majority say they generally are more comfortable as followers than leaders. If you were not one of the first teachers in your school to develop a classroom Web site, but you were in the first half, you are probably a member of the early majority.

Rogers uses the term *skeptical* to describe members of the *late majority.* This group (at 34%, about the same size as the early majority) adopts innovations only with great

Figure 4.1 Categories of Innovativeness (Adapted from Rogers, 1995, p. 262)

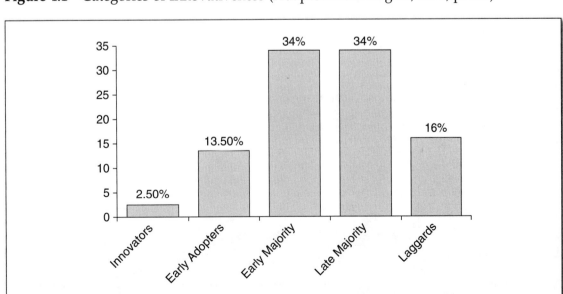

caution. Sometimes seen as set in their ways, they are better understood as people who are uncomfortable with the uncertainty that accompanies most change. Cristina, the speech therapist quoted at the beginning of this chapter, is probably a member of the late majority. Members of this group may change out of necessity, as might happen when a teacher returns to graduate school for a second certification because she needs to insure job security. Or they may change as a result of pressure from their peers, for example, when most teachers want to adopt an interdisciplinary structure or a common set of behavioral expectations. Change is reluctantly agreed to by members of the late majority, and they may hold out for a while, hoping that the change will be reversed.

Those in the last group to adopt an innovation are called *laggards*. Rogers describes people in this group, which comprises about 16% of the population, as *traditional*. Unconvinced that innovation represents improvement, they prefer to stay with policies and practices that have been successful in the past. If you are still using a typewriter, while all the other teachers in your school are using computers, you are likely to be a member of this group. Although the term *laggard* seems belittling, members of this group play an important role in preserving traditional values and calling attention to flaws in an innovation. They often enable others to critically examine a change and prevent an innovation from being adopted prior to a thorough review.

It's been nearly 40 years since Rogers first identified these categories, and others have verified their usefulness in fields as diverse as public health information, telecommunications and mobile technology, independent films distribution, development of new pharmaceuticals, environmentally sound design and building practices, and promotion and marketing of new consumer products (Rogers, 1995). Complete Change Challenge 4.1 to see if the categories help you understand how you respond to the introduction of an innovation.

Change Challenge 4.1 Locating Yourself on the Continuum

Recall the last time you were asked to adopt a new policy or practice at school. Which category is the best match for how you responded?

- Does this category reflect how you usually respond? If not, which category is the best match for your *typical* response?

  _____

  _____

  _____

- Is your typical response to innovation the same in your personal life as in your professional life?

  _____

  _____

  _____

- Are you comfortable with your typical response, or would you prefer to be more or less cautious when you encounter an innovation?

  _____

  _____

  _____

Innovation represents an important kind of change in education, but it is only one among the many changes teachers experience. Whether faced with implementing an innovation or with adjusting to any of the other changes we considered in Chapter 2 (e.g., new position, new administration), the simple fact is sometimes our first response is to resist.

UNDERSTANDING RESISTANCE TO CHANGE

> If I had been there thousands of years ago when somebody invented the wheel, I would have said, "Don't!"
>
> —Pete Seeger, musician and activist, quoted
> in Lipstein, 2007, p. 52

Do teachers resist change? Of course we do; it is part of the human condition. Even Pete Seeger, a champion of social change for almost 70 years, acknowledges that his first response to the prospect of change is resistance. Hardwired into all of us as a way to preserve whatever security and success we enjoy, resistance to change is as inevitable as change itself (Hall & Hord, 2001).

It's unfortunate that the phrase *resistance to change* has a mostly negative connotation, bringing to mind people who are stubbornly old-fashioned (and probably cantankerous, to boot). But just as change isn't always good, resistance isn't always bad. Resistance, which is usually an early response, is sometimes a wise one. Most important, it is a response we can move beyond if we choose.

Teachers have a reputation for being excessively resistant to change (e.g., Hohn, 1998; Richardson, 1998). As we explained in Chapter 1, most of the educational literature on change is directed at school administrators who are charged with bringing about change in teachers' behavior (e.g., Richards, 2002; Zimmerman, 2006). Teachers may be seen as resistant to change primarily by those who are accountable for making sure the change occurs. Richardson and Placier (2001) describe what usually happens: "Someone outside the classroom holds power over change, and teachers are often characterized as recalcitrant and resistant when they do not implement the change suggested" (p. 906).

Our study corroborates the observations Richardson (1998) made a decade earlier: Teachers readily engage in voluntary change. Our survey and interview data also document the extent to which teachers successfully navigate change they did not choose for themselves. Nevertheless, teachers—like people everywhere—at times resist change.

Resistance We Should Resolve

When we are faced with mandatory, top-down change,[1] we may feel that the combination of circumstances with which we're trying to cope defies neat categorization and makes attempts to analyze our resistance seem simpleminded. Nevertheless, people who

---

[1] See Chapter 3 for detailed discussion of "top-down" change within educational settings.

have studied the change process (see, for example, Jick & Peiperl, 2003) notice that most resistance can be traced to a few common roots.

Failure to Be Convinced

Administrators who are respectful of teachers' professionalism routinely share the reasons behind their requests and recommendations. However, teachers may resist change when they cannot see the need for it. If we have not heard compelling arguments or seen convincing data, it makes no sense to abandon practices we know to be useful, simply because someone (usually someone removed from the day-to-day work of teaching) tells us to.

> Our school is in a poor, rural community, and doing well in school is not high on the agenda for most families in our district. We're not being difficult, we're just being realistic when we accept that our kids are never going to do really well on the state tests. But when the results [from the statewide standardized testing program] were published in the paper, and we all saw how badly our kids did compared to [a neighboring district], which is no better off economically, it was a wake-up call. We knew we had to change; if they could do it, so could we.
>
> —Greta, middle school English teacher

Change Challenge 4.2 | Questions for Reflection

Before assuming a change is unnecessary, ask yourself the following:

- How carefully have I considered the rationale for the proposed change?
- If I believe that the information provided is insufficient to convince me that a change is needed, where can I look for more information?
- What data would satisfy me that the change is likely to represent an improvement?
- What is the timeline for getting involved? Is it possible to wait until data are available?
- What evidence is there that the status quo is satisfactory and no change is needed?

Habit

It is easy to see why habit is an obstacle to change and a source of resistance: It's simply easier and more comfortable to keep doing things as we've always done them, thus avoiding the disruption a change would bring. It would be wrong, however, to see habit as little more than inertia. Classrooms are complex environments, with lots going on simultaneously. To meet the challenge of managing them, we need to become adept at multitasking, and to do that, we develop routines and procedures that allow us to be efficient. We know the pleasure that comes from seeing a well-managed class that seems to run itself; that phenomenon wouldn't be possible if it weren't for processes that have become habitual, for ourselves and our students. When a proposed change threatens to interfere with the habits that allow us to manage our classes effectively, resistance is understandable.

Change Challenge 4.3	Questions for Reflection

Before seeing change as a threat to the learning environment you have created, ask the following:

- How much of my resistance is rooted in dismay at the prospect of the hard work I will have to undertake to develop new habits and routines that are necessary to make my life as a teacher manageable?
- What is the probability that, having developed effective habits once, I'll be able to do so again, and perhaps more easily this time?
- At what point does the tinkering needed to make familiar routines fit changed circumstances become more work than it's worth?

Fear of Loss

Even when we recognize the potential for improvement that a change promises, we may still find ourselves reluctant to abandon our familiar ways. This form of resistance is rooted in grieving over what we know we must give up in order to adopt the change. Often we stand to lose much more than mere routines. If we change grade levels, we will have to mothball treasured units that took us years to perfect. We will have to set aside meticulously planned strategies for teaching complex concepts that brought us the sweet sound of "Aaahhhh!" If we change schools, we risk losing relationships with colleagues who have become friends and who have helped us mark the milestones in our personal and professional lives.

Fear of Failure

Education is a public venue; if we fail at change, it will not remain a secret. Further, because most change is mandated from the top, failing at change carries a risk of punishment (Roettger, 2006; Quinn, 1996). Troubling as these consequences are, they pale in comparison to the risk of losing our identity as competent teachers, skilled at helping students learn. There is one simple fact that drives our use of our current teaching strategies: We have seen that they work. We cannot be certain that we will be as successful with a new curriculum, a different teaching partner, or a more challenging group of students (Guskey, 2002). We dread returning to the struggles we had as beginning teachers, when we invested so much time and energy in lessons that sometimes failed miserably. Our resistance to change may be an attempt to avoid the loss of student learning—and of our own self-esteem—that will result when we find ourselves fumbling to rescue a faltering lesson, unable to call on the expertise we used to prize.

Resistance of this sort can be intensified if administrators introduce the change ineptly. As one teacher wrote, "Many times the changes are presented in such a way that I feel like we are dumping all the 'old' in favor of the new. As if all we've done in the past is wrong, ineffective, and stupid" (Richards, 2002, p. 77).

Change Challenge 4.4	Questions for Reflection

Reluctant to let go of what works? Try asking yourself the following:

- How much of my resistance is not a rejection of the new but a desire to hang on to the tried-and-true?
- Is allegiance to colleagues and friends at the heart of my resistance?
- Could my resistance be an expression of protest against the way the change is being handled?
- Am I forgetting that I will be bringing into the changed circumstances all of the knowledge and skills and all of the personal and professional qualities that helped me to create the situation I am so reluctant to part with now?

Negative Experiences

Sometimes resistance to change is a consequence of the failure of earlier change efforts. As Mike Schmoker (1999) says, "Umpteen reforms have come and gone, using up time, money, and hope. They have left a crippling disillusionment in their wake, a cynicism about [any belief that change] benefits students" (p. 37).

While such disillusionment and cynicism may be understandable as sources of resistance, they are also regrettable. They can contribute to a pervasive jadedness that is damaging to both teachers and students. This can be seen in a comment from a teacher who completed our survey. When asked what advice she would give to teachers facing a change, this 20-year veteran of elementary classrooms wrote, "Remember whole language? Well, whatever it is you are facing: this, too, shall pass." Few of us would want our sons and daughters assigned to a teacher with this attitude toward change.

Change Challenge 4.5	Questions for Reflection

If you are feeling disillusioned about educational change in general, ask the following:

- To what extent have my prior experiences with change led to pessimistic expectations that are discouraging me from investigating the proposed change on its own merits?
- Am I generalizing unfairly, by ascribing to either the proposed change or the change agent's negative attributes that characterized a previous (perhaps unrelated) change?
- What can I do to regain the optimistic outlook and the openness to growth and development that propelled me into teaching in the first place?

Resistance We Should Respect

The sources of resistance described above—failure to see a need for change, habit, fear of loss, fear of failure, and prior negative experiences—are ones we should seek to resolve. We do not want to let them stand in the way of a change that we recognize is good or hamper our adjustment to a change that is inevitable.

There are times, however, when teachers' resistance to change should not be viewed as just an obstacle to be overcome. It can be an important element in the change process, providing another layer of scrutiny before a change can affect students.

> [We] advised leaders in education to take a less stigmatizing and dismissive approach to teacher resistance to change. We urged more empathy with "resistant" teachers because their cautiousness about investing in change was often a rational response to bad changes. . . . Resisters may be right. They have "good sense" in seeing through the change as faddish, misdirected, ideological, or unworkable (Gitlin and Margonis, 1995). At the very least their perspective on change will be different and divergent from yours. Quell resistance and you remove the opportunities for change. (Hargreaves & Fullan, 1998, p. 120)

At times, resistance is even a teacher's ethical obligation. In this final section of the chapter we see resistance as a warning signal to considering doing things differently.

Pragmatic Concerns

Most of us have the firsthand experience of solving one problem only to unintentionally create a new one. For example, when Kathy and Yessenia finally managed to rewrite a class play so that all students in their inclusive class had meaningful roles, they were faced with a new problem: not enough space in the classroom for all the family members who wanted to see their children perform. Of course they didn't cancel the play or return to a more traditional play format; instead, having made one good change, they then had to make another to insure the success of the first, by working with their principal to find an alternate performance space.

Similar unforeseen circumstances can damage major change efforts, especially when teachers do not have a voice in planning for the change. "Too often, teachers who are going through the change process are not consulted on the usefulness of the innovation, yet are expected to adopt it with open arms" (Donovan, Hartley, & Strudler, 2007, p. 279). Teachers who hesitate under these circumstances should not be regarded as merely resistant; they might be an important early warning system.

I supported our new elementary principal's desire to move toward an integrated curriculum for Grades 4, 5, and 6. But I didn't think we were ready to make the move so quickly. We still had to use the report card that was common to the district's five elementary schools, and that had a subject-based format. In fact, it had been revised a couple of years before to align with the state-mandated testing program, which was also subject based. So clearly it wasn't going to change any time soon. I guess our principal just hadn't gotten that far in her thinking. I sensed she was annoyed with me, because she thought she could count on me as an ally. But I couldn't just sit there with my mouth shut. I could see what would happen down the line.

—Luz, veteran fifth-grade teacher

Philosophical Disagreements

Finally, teachers should resist change that they believe will have a negative effect on student learning. As Hargreaves, Earl, Moore, and Manning (2001) point out,

> Not all change is good. Educational reform is sometimes superficial, driven by political popularity and economic stringency rather than educational values. It can be harmful to less successful students. It can also destroy working conditions that enable teachers to do their jobs well. (p. 121)

Teachers who have genuine philosophical disagreements with the change, based on their professional knowledge of children's development and learning, must be encouraged to speak up. Guidance on how to advocate effectively against a proposed change that is not in students' best interests, and moral support for doing so, is often available from teachers' professional organizations, such as the National Council of Teachers of English (NCTE), National Council of Teachers of Mathematics (NCTM), American Association for the Education of Young Children (AAEYC), and the Council for Exceptional Children (CEC), among others.

Analyzing One Teacher's Resistance to Change

Distressed by the prospect of an involuntary transfer to a new assignment, Anne resisted strenuously. As you read her account, try to identify the sources of her resistance.

When I was transferred to the high school, I went kicking and screaming. This was not the job I had applied for, not the job I wanted, and certainly not one I would be good at. I had taught for four years in a self-contained K–2 class for students with moderate disabilities. I loved the kids, most of whom had Down's syndrome, and I had developed great relationships with their families. I got along well with my aide, and getting to that point had definitely not been easy. I counted among the other teachers several personal friends, including a few older faculty members I felt I could go to for help without feeling like I was betraying my stupidity. So I was devastated when the director of special education told me, in June, that I would be switching positions with the high school resource teacher.

The high school resource teacher hated the idea as much as I did, but everybody knew why they were doing it. To put it bluntly, nothing much was happening in that high school program. Attendance was atrocious, achievement was worse, and the dropout rate was a disgrace. The kids pushed every boundary, and she simply caved in. When I visited the class, I almost cried. Every desk and chair in the room, every bulletin board, even the chalkboard, was damaged. There was a hole in the wall where one of the kids had thrown a chair.

I did everything I could to reverse the decision. I went to the union, to my building principal, even to the superintendent. (I didn't ask the parents to go to bat for me, but I was tempted.) I argued that while I could teach reading and math to young children with cognitive deficits, I was far from prepared to teach algebra and earth science to adolescents with behavior problems. I pleaded for time to nurture the cross-age tutoring program I had begun, which was beginning to open up some very traditional teachers to working in not-so-traditional ways. I even confessed to having hated high school myself, and to dreading the return to a place where I never felt comfortable.

None of it helped. Basically, the administration had the right to assign me to any class covered by my certification, and they went ahead and did it. I was in no position to look for another job, since that would mean giving up tenure and all of my accumulated sick leave, and my husband and I were hoping to start a family soon. I felt powerless, resentful, and depressed.

I tell this story to every one of my student teachers, because they can learn a lot from it. It has a happy ending. It took a while, but I fell in love with teaching older kids. I've taught grades 7–12 ever since, and I can't see myself going back to an elementary position. I love the vitality and energy of this age group, and I love their sense of humor. I like the variety in the secondary content areas. I'm also motivated by the sense that "the buck stops here." If I can't reach them, they just might fall off the map. It is easy to see that I make a difference.

—Anne, secondary special education teacher

You probably inferred that Anne understood the need for a change in the high school program. You may also have noticed that Anne doesn't mention any pragmatic concerns or philosophical differences that would account for her resistance. What's perfectly clear is that Anne did not want to leave students she enjoyed and colleagues she valued at the elementary school, and that she doubted her ability to be successful in the high school. Anne's resistance seems to have been rooted in fear of loss and fear of failure.

Change Challenge 4.6   Analyzing Resistance

- Spend a few minutes recalling a time in your teaching career when you were apprehensive about a change you were facing. For now, focus on your feelings just before and in the early stages of the change.
- Consider again the sources of resistance described in this chapter: habit, or the preference for familiar ways of doing things; fear of loss; fear of failure; negative experiences with other changes; practical concerns about implementing the change; and philosophical disagreement with the change. Identify the one or two sources of resistance that were strongest for you at the time.

_____

_____

_____

(Continued)

(Continued)

- With the magical gift of hindsight (20/20, of course), assess the extent to which your resistance was warranted. Were the old habits particularly hard to give up? Did your fears of loss or failure materialize? Was the implementation as rocky as you predicted? Were there unfortunate consequences to student learning?

  _____

  _____

  _____

- Imagine that the older and wiser person you are today could offer words of guidance and support to the younger and less experienced person you were then. What would you say to ease the apprehension that faced you then?

  _____

  _____

  _____

- What personal strengths would you point to as resources to use in navigating the change?

  _____

  _____

  _____

- Look ahead to a change you are likely to encounter in the next three years. (If you're not sure what lies ahead, see Chapter 2 to review the changes teachers typically encounter in their careers.) Try to predict the type of resistance you are most likely to experience. Based on the insights you have gained from this chapter, write three reminders to yourself about understanding resistance and choosing how you will address it.

  1.

  2.

  3.

Looking Ahead

In Chapter 4, we have seen that people vary in how we approach change, and sometimes our first response is resistance. Examining the reasons for our resistance enables us to alter our response if we choose. In Chapter 5, we will explore what happens when, ready or not, we experience change. We will look at two different models that describe the stages of the change process.

CHAPTER 5

Charting the Stages
of Change

Anyone who has tried to get rid of clutter "once and for all," or vowed to eat only wholesome foods "from now on" has learned that change just doesn't work that way. *Change is a process, not an event.* But often we forget what Bridges (2004) and Hall and Hord (2001) point out: Change is never a one-shot deal; it is a developmental process. It takes time, and we have to make adjustments and accommodations along the way.

In this chapter, we will look at how our thoughts and feelings shift as the change process unfolds. We'll begin by summarizing the work of Frances Fuller, who identified *stages of concern* for teachers. Then we'll look at William Bridges's three-phase model of life's transitions, which is useful in understanding the changes we experience both at school and at home. We'll use a series of exercises to reflect on our past experiences with change so we can better understand each phase in the process. Knowing what to expect as we begin a new endeavor—whether or not it is of our own choosing—can help us navigate change successfully.

TEACHERS' CONCERNS EVOLVE
DURING THE CHANGE PROCESS

Gene Hall and Shirley Hord have devoted their careers to understanding how teachers respond to change, especially the changes that are instituted as part of reform efforts. They have found that "there is a developmental pattern to how our feelings and perceptions evolve as the change process unfolds" (Hall & Hord, 2001, p. 57). Their studies have shown that teachers' concerns about change parallel closely the concerns that they experienced while becoming teachers. Those stages were first described by Frances Fuller (Fuller, 1969; Fuller & Brown, 1975), whose work is now considered classic.

Spurred by uneven course evaluations from students in one of her courses at the University of Texas at Austin, Fuller tried to determine why some students found the course helpful and others most definitely did not. She learned that students who had some experiences working with children, perhaps as parents or Sunday school teachers, gave the course higher ratings. She realized that they saw the course as addressing their concerns, while other students described the course as irrelevant. Fuller then undertook a systematic study of the concerns teachers experience in the process of becoming teachers. The concerns she identified have since been found to apply to professional development in fields other than education, such as medicine and physical therapy (Hall & Hord, 2001).

Stages of Concern

Fuller and her colleagues identified four *stages of concern*. The first stage, *unrelated concerns,* is experienced primarily by those who are just beginning to learn about their chosen field, rather than those actually practicing it. We will focus on the three stages that are relevant for practicing teachers, which are characterized by concerns about *self, task,* and *impact.*

Self Concerns

Concerns about self are natural when people begin to teach. As beginning teachers, we focus on questions like "How will I make it through four periods without a break?" and "What will I do if I can't use the copier to make transparencies?" Hall and Hord found that concerns about self also are natural when teachers feel like beginners all over again, as we do when we are asked to replace instructional strategies that we know how to use effectively with new approaches that feel foreign and strange. We wonder what the change will mean for us personally: Will I be able to do this and do it well? If my principal asks to observe me using the new approach, will the observation go as smoothly as it usually does?

Fuller and Brown (1975) noted that concerns about self are concerns about survival. Mercifully, most of us are absorbed only briefly by self and survival concerns when we begin teaching. By the midpoint of our first year, most of us know we are going to survive and can pay more attention to other concerns. Similarly, experienced teachers soon recognize that we can call on the personal strengths that we have developed through years of teaching to figure out how to make a change work for our students and ourselves.

Task Concerns

As self and survival concerns diminish, concerns about our new tasks increase, for both "beginners" just learning to teach and for "experienced teachers" implementing changes. We become absorbed by the organizational and management burdens of the new undertaking. We focus on finding the right resources—the background information we need, the instructional materials our students will use, the computer technician who will help us with the new software. We rearrange our schedules to accommodate the change, and when chaos ensues, we rearrange them again. Everything takes more time than it should, and we struggle to regain the efficient automaticity that characterized our previous ways of doing things.

Impact Concerns

With time though, we do find ways to manage the new tasks associated with the change. As we become more efficient, we have time and energy to turn our attention to considering the impact of the change. We focus less on ourselves and the tasks we must manage and more on student learning. We notice who is learning and who is struggling. We become preoccupied not with how to juggle new methods and materials, but with how to reach all students and make sure they are learning what we are trying to teach. Ultimately, we ask if the new way of doing things leads to improved learning for our students.

In using the term *stages of concern*, Fuller and Brown imply a developmental sequence, and Hall and Hord (2001) note that quite often the sequence follows a "wave motion" (p. 65). When the change process unfolds as expected, self concerns are the first to be felt, and they are most intense just before the new policy or practice is implemented. As the change gets underway, task concerns come to dominate and self concerns diminish. With time, impact concerns become the major focus, with self and task concerns receding.

Change Challenge 5.1   Identifying the Different Concerns That Emerge in the Change Process

In the paragraphs below, Kim recounts the difficulties she experienced in making a transition to a new math curriculum. As you read, try to spot examples of the *self*, *task*, and *impact concerns* identified by Fuller and Brown, and see if they follow the *wave motion* noted by Hall and Hord.

The year we went to the new math program was a mess. It was completely unreasonable. First we had to come in for workshops during the summer, which felt very presumptuous to me. We got paid, but I resented the school district's expectation that we'd just make ourselves available on their schedule.

But the big problem was the time commitment, which proved to be a problem for the entire year. The curriculum coordinator for math said we had to spend at least 90 minutes a day on math instruction and let us know that our principal was expected to be sure this requirement was being met in all the primary classrooms. Ninety minutes! No normal second-grade teacher spends 90 minutes on math. I had no idea how I was going to find an extra hour in each day to devote to math. What did they think we were doing in second grade, playtime? Naps? My kids' days were already packed. We did great stuff—enriching, authentic, meaningful activities. I got my master's from Bank Street College of Education and I was a Montessori teacher before that; I know what seven-year-olds need. I did not want to toss out things I knew worked and replace them with the unknown. And certainly not for 90 minutes a day.

And then there was all the time I had to spend preparing just to teach math each day. I felt like a first-year teacher all over again—taking home the teacher's manual, finding manipulatives, creating game boards, tinkering with schedules. It was too much. It just took over.

Of course, something had to go. I just couldn't manage to put on the play that year. Parents were disappointed because my class plays were a tradition families looked forward to. Heck, I look forward to them—the play gives everyone a chance to shine. Everybody gets an important role, something that matches their strengths, and I have fun getting to know my students well enough to figure out what that is. But there are only so many hours in the day. I didn't have to do the play, but I did have to get through that math curriculum.

(Continued)

(Continued)

And I did get through it. It's not a bad math program. In many ways it is consistent with what I believe about how kids learn best. Now that we're into the third year, it's fine. But I can't say it is better than what we were doing before, can't say that kids now understand math in some fabulous new way.

- What *self concerns* does Kim express?
- What *task concerns* are evident in her account?
- How does Kim express *impact concerns*?

Kim's account is especially helpful because it illustrates that self, task, and impact concerns do not always occur in the linear, sequential way that developmental stage theories may imply (see Bullough, 1997). For Kim, self concerns occur simultaneously with task concerns; this can be seen as she describes the personal time she had to devote to planning lessons and preparing materials. Her impact concerns emerge not just at the end, as the model implies, but from the very beginning, when she worries that she will be forced to give up activities she knows to be valuable in order to accommodate the new math program. Kim again mentions impact concerns at the end of her account, when she concludes that the new program is not noticeably better than the previous one.

CHANGE OCCURS IN PHASES

William Bridges's work addresses the psychological dimension of change, which he calls "transition" (Bridges, 2004, p. xii), and builds on the classic work of social psychologist Kurt Lewin. Understanding the process of transitions can help people through the major changes in their lives, at home and at work. Bridges has found that adapting to change proceeds in predictable ways for most people, whether the change takes place at home or at work and whether the change is one we chose or one that was imposed. Bridges's accessible model has been a guide for educators (Cramer, 2006) as well as for business leaders (Orr, 2000) and nurses (Thompson & Hammer, 2007). The three transition phases Bridges identifies—an ending, a neutral zone, and a new beginning—are evident in George's account of his return to graduate school.

"Back to School": An Illustration of Change as a Process With Three Phases

My pursuit of an advanced degree was unusual in my school district. "Hey, George," my fellow teachers would say to me, "what are you putting yourself through all that grief for?" They knew that our superintendent had spoken to several of us about picking up a second teaching credential. Our rural district is losing population, and as teachers retire or move out of the area, they are not being replaced. Instead, other teachers are assigned to pick up their courses. So I had to go back to school, whether I wanted to or not. I could have just taken 12 credits to qualify for a new certificate, but I decided to go for a master's instead. I had been getting a little bored with the same classes I had taught for 15 years, so I looked into a totally new subject area for me—technology education. I figured it would keep the superintendent happy, satisfy my hankering for something new, and maybe open up options for me somewhere else. [*Endings*]

When I began taking courses, it hit me—I would be the one receiving (rather than giving out) grades! I got very uneasy about how I would measure up to other graduate students—they were mostly young and several had been using computers since before they could walk. I was going to classes, trying to keep up with the readings and the assignments, but not really learning much. It was an uncomfortable time; I felt like I didn't really belong, and often I asked myself, "What am I doing here?" I stuck it out, but at the time I don't think I could have told you why. Finding a good advisor, and making a few friends, made the difference. [*Neutral zone*]

My new advisor was able to point me toward some excellent resources. I also felt a connection with a couple of other grad students like me, experienced teachers trying to juggle full-time jobs with part-time study. We were able to support each other. My rusty study habits improved, as did my confidence. When the first semester ended and I got my grades, I was very proud of myself. I didn't slide backwards just because not every grade was an A. [*New beginnings*]

—George, veteran physics teacher, newly certified in technology education, now teaching computer graphics

In the remaining sections of this chapter, we'll examine each of the three transition phases. We'll also reflect on our previous experiences with change, trying to see within each the ending, neutral zone, and new beginning. Understanding what we were doing, thinking, and feeling during an earlier change should help us face the next change with greater ease.

An Overview of the Change Process

Instead of thinking of change as a pair of parentheses facing each other, containing the change events

(change)

consider them instead as parentheses facing outward, implying what had taken place in the past, as well as what is yet to come. Between the two outward facing parentheses, the process of change takes place.

past events) change process (*future changes*

Bridges's work draws our attention to all three of these parts of the change process:

Endings: All changes begin with a realization that the status quo is no longer satisfying. Sometimes we are the ones to come to this realization, for example, when we volunteer for a new assignment because our current position is no longer challenging, or when we choose to leave a failing relationship. Sometimes others bring the situation to its end, as when a child goes off to college or a school adopts a new reading series. An important element of this phase is the realization that something will be lost when the change is implemented. In the example above, George realized that he could no longer count on being able to teach physics full time in his current district. The ending he encountered was prompted both by external events—declining enrollments that led to a "request" from the superintendent—and by internal factors, such as George's desire for a graduate degree that could lead to career revitalization.

Neutral Zone: The neutral zone is a moratorium, an often disquieting space in which we are suspended between the old and the new. We may feel like we should be moving ahead, especially if the change is one we initiated or endorse; frustrations under these circumstances can take us by surprise. The neutral zone also is the time when we begin to explore—not always fruitfully—ways to move ahead. In the example above, George unexpectedly found that he didn't relish his new role—he wasn't learning and he felt out of place. He was no longer simply a physics teacher, but not yet really a graduate student either. He looked for ways to ease his discomfort and found them in an advisor and fellow students.

New Beginnings: A new beginning occurs when there is an "internal realignment" (Bridges, 2004, p. 162) and an accompanying motivation to see the change through successfully. There is still a need to make an overt commitment to the change, as the danger of regression is very real. But we are happy to be free of the equivocal status of the neutral zone and ready to take steps, however faltering, toward the new goal. In the example above, finding kindred spirits and acknowledging that he did not need to earn all As helped George make the transition to seeing himself as a successful graduate student.

The following sections of the chapter give you a chance to analyze a change you have gone through and prepare for future changes with the benefits of anticipating what is ahead.

Endings: Recognizing That a Change Is Needed

Change in all settings—professional and personal—is triggered by many different starting points. It is reasonable, though, to see them all as a variation on change originating from *within* or from *without*. The quotes below are taken from teachers' responses to our survey question, "How do you know when you are ready to make a change in your professional life?"

Changes from within are often made in response to feelings of discomfort. The teachers in our study used the terms *bored, apathetic, unchallenged, stagnating,* and *unsatisfied,* and said they no longer found work to be *exciting, stimulating,* or *something to look forward to,* as these quotes from the surveys illustrate:

- "I become bored, and I wonder if I can't make a bigger difference elsewhere."
- "When what you are teaching becomes too routine, and you realize you are on auto-pilot."
- "When you do not feel like you are being effective and stimulating to the students."
- "I love my job, and when that feeling stops, I know a change is necessary."
- "I feel stuck, unhappy, or unchallenged."
- "When it isn't fun anymore."

Changes from within also stem from feelings of competence and mastery. A few teachers said they knew they were ready for a change when they had the sense of being at the top of their game and ready to tackle new challenges:

- "When I feel I have made an impact and am ready to move on to another level."
- "When there are new opportunities to use my strengths and skills in a positive way."
- "When you feel you are at the top of the heap."

Changes from without are sometimes imposed by others, from building principals to state legislators:

- "When the curriculum changes—when a new classroom assignment or state regulations change."
- "Most of the time, changes are imposed on me, by new regulations, new administration, or other staff that I am working with. I have rarely initiated changes on my own."

Changes from without also can be those we choose to make in response to changes in the environment, when we reflect on our teaching and find opportunities for improvement:

- "When alumni return to visit and tell me what prepared them and what didn't prepare them for college."
- "When I begin to see that very little change will occur or has occurred to bring positive influences to bear on the climate or morale of the school in which I am teaching."
- "Changes in my professional life have typically been dictated by the situation. A negative environment forced me to leave a school. Just as much as a positive approach has caused me to recognize the power of adapting or changing to welcome a new situation or approach."

In the quotes above, teachers have pointed out the signs that tell them it is time to do something different, either within their current setting or elsewhere. Bridges (2004) identifies a few other feelings that we may encounter in the endings phase: a sense of *panic* when we recognize that we can no longer do what we have done; *disenchantment* that things are not as good as we hoped they would be; and *disorientation,* or the feeling of being confused about how things stand and unsure of what happens next.

Consider the complex emotions felt by Julio, a middle school social studies teacher, as he realized that one phase of his life was coming to an end.

Julio's Story

Phase I: Endings

Like everyone else I know, I remember where I was on September 11, 2001. I was home alone, recovering from surgery. As I watched the events on television, I felt overwhelmed not only by the horror of what was happening, but by the realization that my students were probably witnessing it too and would be even more bewildered and frightened than I. As their teacher, it would be my responsibility to help them process it. But if I could not even comprehend it for myself, how could I help them to make sense of it?

(Continued)

(Continued)

That evening, as I searched the Internet for guidance about how to help my students, my 18-year-old brother called to tell me he had enlisted in the Marines. For once, the students in my classes weren't my first priority—my "little" brother was. I could hardly think straight, worrying about what we could do to keep him safe. My family and I tried to get him to reverse his enlistment, or at least to transfer to a branch of service where he would be less in harm's way, but we were powerless to change his mind.

When I returned to school, the teaching of social studies had taken on a new urgency for me.

World events led to an ending of feelings of safety and security within Julio's family and to changed relationships; inevitably, these would have an impact on Julio's life at school too. Take some time to reflect back on a change you have experienced and complete the exercise below.

Change Challenge 5.2 | Endings

For the purposes of this Change Challenge, reflect upon a *completed* change that you initiated. Select a change in either your personal or professional life (for example, moving to a new residence, or volunteering for a new grade level). It can be one you undertook with enthusiasm, such as getting married, or with regret, such as ending a problematic relationship. If you need a jump start, review the changes described in Chapter 2.

In hindsight, what signs were there that something was *ending* for you?

- Did you begin to see flaws in the situation you were in, or doubt your ability to thrive in it?
- Did you have the sense that things could be better, an idea about what could change, perhaps a sense of optimism?
- Did you find your thoughts returning to the situation more than usual, or talk about it more with friends and family, or try to clarify your ideas by writing them down?
- Whatever happened, record what became for you signs of an *ending*.

_____

_____

_____

In the endings phase, there is usually a blend of optimism and anxiety, feelings and thoughts that are challenging us to look at our situation in new ways. As we find ourselves in a situation in which there are few clear resources to use, we must move on to the next stage of the change process, the *neutral zone*.

The Neutral Zone: Preparing to Change

It would be great if recognizing that we need to do something different, to change some aspect of our lives, would lead directly to a new and different dynamic. Observing people in transition has led Bridges to conclude that between the recognition that we need to change and the actual beginning of the new endeavor, we pass through what he calls a neutral zone, an "apparently unproductive time out," a time of "attentive inactivity and ritualized routine" (Bridges, 2004, p. 135). We feel that we are stalled when we should be making progress. Bridges counsels, though, that this is a moratorium with an important purpose, which is to figure out what it is we really want from the next stage. The comment below suggests that the teacher was in the midst of the neutral zone when she wrote it:

- "The death of my mother sent me into a life change. Along with the depression, I am rethinking my life's purpose. I don't feel like I fit into the school system, or even daily life. I know more than ever now what I want—a better quality of daily life and more time for my family."

The neutral zone might aptly be named the "trial and error" zone, because it is here that we make our mistakes. An educator once said that unless you double your mistakes each year, you aren't really trying. Robert Kennedy said the same thing, slightly differently: "Only those who dare to fail greatly can ever achieve greatly." We'd like to be assured that after years of teaching, we would become more, rather than less, proficient, and that we'd learn to avoid mistakes. But Kennedy's recommendation to keep stretching and reaching encourages us to continue to attempt not just the safe, predictable things, but to take up new challenges as well. It's a good recommendation to keep in mind as we cope with the false starts and near misses of the neutral zone.

Consider how the neutral zone felt to Julio, whose brother enlisted after September 11, 2001.

Julio's Story

Phase II: The Neutral Zone

Unfortunately, despite my resolve, the events of 9–11 did not lead to the change in my teaching that I had expected. None of the students in our school were directly impacted, so our discussions about what happened were fairly factual.

Even after U.S. troops were sent to Iraq several months later, I did not know what to do. My role as a brother of a Marine was complicated enough: I joined marches protesting the war, but I also put "support our troops" ribbons on my car. But what was the appropriate role for me as a teacher? Other schools were organizing "teach-ins" on the Muslim world, but I did not have the knowledge or skills to do that. The fading maps of the Middle East I had tacked up in September were reminders that I wanted to do something. But anything I thought of seemed like a feeble and inadequate response to the most enormous event of my lifetime.

An idea I kept circling back to was getting my students involved in some way with our troops. At first I figured anything we did would be directed to my brother's unit. I had no idea what we could do that would really help, so I talked with some teachers who were veterans. They put me in touch with members of our local VFW. Talking to them helped me realize that we needed to think beyond my brother and his buddies.

(Continued)

(Continued)

Finally, I decided to bring the topic up with my classes. I wasn't sure this was a good idea—emotions were running high in our town. But I thought we would be OK if we kept ourselves focused on letting the troops overseas know that the people back home remembered them. Anyway, good idea or not, after so many months I was finally ready to do something; doing nothing was draining my batteries.

Julio's account conveys the unsettled aimlessness that is characteristic of the neutral zone. It also highlights a number of strategies we can use to find our way through it:

- Seek additional information
- Generate alternatives
- Patiently try out different possibilities
- Learn to live with uneasiness of this fallow stage

Change Challenge 5.3   The Neutral Zone

Think back to the change you chose to reflect on in Change Challenge 5.2. What was your neutral zone like? Was it a time of unproductive inactivity? Do you recall feelings of emptiness or aimlessness? Try to find words to capture what the experience felt like to you.

_____

_____

_____

_____

What did you do to try to move beyond the neutral zone? Did you talk to people you thought could help? Consider new, even outlandish, possibilities? Make some attempts at a new start, only to see them fizzle out? Did you then try again? Were you able to be patient with yourself during this awkward period? Record strategies you tried during the time you were making a transition from the old to the new.

_____

_____

_____

_____

How do we know when we are through the neutral zone? Eventually, one of our attempts to do something to break out of it will click—and we are on our way to a new beginning.

New Beginnings: Moving Ahead With Change

As we get to the other side of the neutral zone, we may be looking forward to jumping feet first into the new experience, maybe even making a splash. Well, that doesn't usually happen. Most new beginnings are "indirect, unimpressive, (and) . . . untidy" (Bridges, 2004, p. 158). Instead of fanfare, there are subtle signs that we have begun to think differently, to focus with optimism on the future. A first task of a new beginning is saying good-bye to the kinds of things that we would have done in the past and acknowledging that there are things about them that we will miss. We then need to undertake the process of developing the understandings and skills we'll need to succeed with our change. We also need to make a firm commitment to the new situation, agreeing to stick with it even when it is difficult, as Julio and his students did.

Julio's Story

Phase III: New Beginnings

The kids were responsive during the class discussions about how we could show support for the troops. Most were quiet and thoughtful. They came up with good ideas: collecting different first-aid items or toiletries; having a book drive and sending the books to the troops; collecting personal clothes (underwear, pajamas) and sending them to national distribution centers rather than sending them directly to the troops. From some of their comments, I could see that they were more attuned to what was happening than I expected. For example, they brought up the idea of sending things the troops could distribute to Iraqi school children.

After considering all the options, and weighing the pros and cons, we decided to go with a letter-writing campaign via e-mail. We had a lot of details to work out, but my brother helped me from overseas. Eventually, we got things underway and developed a system.

- We partnered up those students who were able to think of things to write easily with others who had more difficulty.
- Eventually, we kept a log of topics to consider when writing the letters.
- We found the students in the class who were best at correcting grammatical errors, and made sure the letters went to those students before we sent off our e-mails.
- We shared highlights from the responses we received from soldiers on our classroom Web site.

The students were motivated, and very proud of their work.

And then one of our soldiers died. We all felt the loss. Some students didn't want to go on with the project any more—especially Herman, who had been that soldier's e-mail partner. We felt discouraged, as if we should not get our hopes up, should stop sending along encouraging words to our troops.

But one student had the idea to invite some returning soldiers to speak to us. Although the ones who came had not been part of our project, they delivered a compelling message about how much support from home meant. We learned from them that the effort we had put into the project was worth it. Even though the soldiers hadn't always told us, our communications really had made a difference.

Julio's story reminds us that new beginnings do not go smoothly, and that there will be events that tempt us to just drop the whole thing. Julio called on outside resources, who encouraged his students stay with their project through these predictable setbacks.

Change Challenge 5.4 | New Beginnings

Think back to the change experience you've used in the previous two exercises.

- How did you expect the change to proceed?

  _____

  _____

  _____

- How was that different from what actually happened?

  _____

  _____

  _____

- What obstacles and setbacks did you encounter?

  _____

  _____

  _____

- What did you say to encourage yourself when times were tough or progress was sluggish?

  _____

  _____

  _____

- What did you do to celebrate small steps toward your goals?

  _____

  _____

  _____

Looking Ahead

Because change is a process, not an event, our experience of it is continually evolving. Understanding the process and knowing what we might expect at different stages can make the experience easier. In Part III of *A Teacher's Guide to Change*, our focus shifts to the changes that teachers can take charge of, and we offer guidance for planning and carrying out a change effort.

PART III

Implementing Change

Part III of *A Teacher's Guide to Change* highlights the steps teachers use to plan for and implement changes that are fully within a teacher's purview, changes that do not require the approval of an administrator or cooperation of colleagues. In Chapter 6, we outline the details involved in planning for change and ask readers to reflect on personal events outside the classroom. These can be resources for insights to facilitate the change process. In Chapter 7, we provide specific guidance for teachers who are ready to begin something new—either voluntarily or because of a mandate.

Using Personal Experiences to Prepare for Professional Changes

I n the classic movie *Citizen Kane*, the opening scene reveals the end of the story. After a short time, the soundtrack brings us back to the beginning, and we learn how the story unfolded. We are given a seemingly linear progression of events.

Although we don't have panoramic shots or musical accompaniments for our own experiences, using a filmmaker's methods, we could each create a logically sequenced depiction of our own lives. When looking back at our jobs or our romances (those that have been satisfying as well as those that shortchanged us), we can see the logic of (or the fatal mistake in) the preceding events. In retrospect, choices look very different from how they appear when we are in the middle of the decision-making process. Learning to make wise choices is one of the skills that can enable us to do our best with regard to making and sustaining change.

How do we examine our options while we are in the midst of making important choices? To avoid random or coincidental decisions, we must teach ourselves these essential skills, so that our choices are no longer arbitrary or following the path of least resistance. Watson and Tharp's classic text (1977) describes the purposeful process of making personal, intentional choices. This chapter highlights the intentionality they described and invites you to develop a sequenced approach toward the change initiatives you would like to introduce into your future. This chapter will enable you to plan for the changes you would like to introduce into your work. You won't be waiting to see how some important scenes of your life's movie turn out—instead, you will be in charge of them.

DRAWING ON PERSONAL EXPERIENCES

To educate ourselves in the change process, we should make use of all of the resources available to us, including our personal histories. Jersild (2003) examined the emotional responses of teachers who were in the process of self-inquiry, which led to improved work with students. Teachers, busy with curricular requirements and schedule challenges, may ignore the resources that personal life events provide—intellectual and emotional depth of experience that can become part of what we do within our classrooms. What we bring to our work is the ability to make use of our personal interests, strengths, and enthusiasms, leading to being more generous and capable when interacting with others within our school settings.

Bringing the personal together with the professional can connect us with others. Sergiovanni (2000), in discussing the development of the learning community, identifies how teachers connect with each other via shared relationships and shared memories. Sometimes our sharing is based on communal experiences and "is often enshrined in its symbols, traditions, rites, and rituals" (p. 67). But learning communities also are strengthened when members share what they have done individually. How we communicate what is important to us in professional settings can be influenced by what we have experienced in our personal lives. How we cope privately can inform what we do within our school, as this example shows.

Giving Others What I Did Not Get Myself

My personal experience within my family led me to see some of my students' experiences with loss differently than most people. When I was 12 years old, my mother died. I did not get help or counseling then and struggled with emotional issues for most of my life. I was very reluctant to examine how my mother's absence changed my childhood.

Then one of my students lost her father to cancer, and I realized that an event in my past which I'd always kept private could be a resource for me to help my student. With the help of our school psychologist, I sought out and received counseling. I eventually got to the point where I could mine my experience in a totally new way—working with others in our school to put together a handbook for students on bereavement and grief.

Our rural school district suffered a severe loss when one of our sixth-grade students committed suicide. Instead of backing away from the subject, the thinking and work I had done enabled our tiny district to experience this tragedy together. Although I wouldn't have chosen these events to ever take place, I know that I have been changed forever by what happened to me, in ways that enable me to support others experiencing profound losses.

—Keisha, completing her seventh year teaching music in a rural school district

Because this teacher was able to make a decision to change her thinking about her mother's death and decided to direct her energies into assisting students in her school, she achieved a pair of goals. She was able to face an episode in her past that had been inaccessible to her previously, and she was instrumental in enabling members of her district to support students. Langley, O'Connor, and Welkener (2004) recommend the various combinations of private and public reflection and performance as four different ways to develop ourselves. Keisha's example above illustrates how private reflection can emerge in a public way, one that can benefit us personally and also help our students. This section of the chapter lays out a process you can use to capitalize on something that happened to you outside of school, as a resource base for professional changes.

When we examine the change process within our personal lives, we see that we have a surprising number of resources on which to draw. We have experienced predictable changes, such as moving from middle school to high school, learning to drive, or selecting a major in college. Most of us have also been caught off guard by unexpected changes, such as the illness of a family member, unforeseen expectations placed on us outside work, or a sudden need to change our living arrangements. These experiences have given us useful practice in adjusting to change, and we can call on what we have learned through them the next time we face unexpected change.

This section of this chapter is designed to enable you to (1) revisit a successful personal change you accomplished, (2) identify the skills you used in that situation, (3) describe the obstacles that got in your way and how you overcame them, and (4) decide how these skills might be of use to you in professional circumstances. Consider selecting something that you intentionally chose to do, as illustrated in the example below.

I'm Over the Hurdle!

When I turned 30, I decided it was time for me to do something different in my personal life. I've always been nervous about my ability to speak in public among adults. It is so strange that this problem was nonexistent in my classroom—with my students, words come so easily! But at teacher inservices, team meetings, or any situation with more than four adults, my heart would begin to pound and I couldn't find the right words. I enviously watched other people get up and talk—it looked so easy.

I decided that the summer of my 30th year, this would have to change! I joined a local group that specialized in helping people learn to become more at ease with public speaking. I learned some of the tricks that others used, how to prepare, and how to give myself confidence before, during, and after my comments. The result—I'm still nervous on the inside, but I focus on the spot in the room that is likely to give me most support. If it is a smiling person, that is great. It might be the doorframe, or the window, if no one is smiling. But I give myself the applause afterwards, as well as credit for conquering my fears. My experience at our faculty and team meetings has been totally changed. I expected everyone to notice, but strangely—no one said a word. I think this was much bigger in my own mind than it was in the minds of other people.

—Karl, assistant basketball coach and sixth-grade social studies teacher

---

As you look back over the past five years, consider the ways in which you have intentionally changed in your personal life—either to pursue a new goal, or to rectify a problem situation. Consider including a wide circle of experiences outside of your professional life, including your family, friendships, living circumstances, hobbies, and pursuit of learning that is separate from your professional development. The list below contains personal changes that members of our research project identified as being useful as resources for professional changes. Perhaps one of them will remind you of a personal change you made—either because you wanted to, or because you had to.

- Changes in family circumstances (adult family of choice)
  - Getting engaged or making a commitment to a serious relationship
  - Getting married

- o Becoming a parent
- o Having a child diagnosed with a disability
- o Death of a spouse or child
- o Illness of spouse or child
- o Ending a problematic relationship
- o Coming close to bankruptcy
- o Buying a house

- Changes in family circumstances (family of origin)

  - o Improving relationships with family members as everyone in the family ages
  - o Illness of a parent
  - o Death of a parent
  - o Remarriage of a parent
  - o Marriage or parenthood of sibling(s)
  - o Aging or death of extended family member(s)

- Changes in career

  - o Leaving teaching for a time
  - o Changing grade level or content specialization
  - o Returning to teaching after raising children
  - o Moving to a new district
  - o District undergoing changes that impact teachers

- Change in outlook or style

  - o Learning to laugh
  - o Becoming more empathetic, especially with students
  - o Seeking support from others during difficult time
  - o Becoming more patient
  - o Translating parenting skills into classroom practices
  - o Becoming a senior member of the faculty
  - o Achieving professional recognition

Consider the following set of Change Challenges as a way to look back on *one personal change you have already **successfully** accomplished*. This reflection has been designed to assist you in preparing to examine a professional change.

Change Challenge 6.1   Reviewing the Start of a *Successfully* Completed Personal Change

Revisit a successful personal change you accomplished by doing the following:

Recall your thoughts and feelings at the outset of your personal change, considering both your intellectual and emotional states.

Mentally review what you hoped to accomplish when you began, and assess how well those hopes matched up with the eventual outcome.

> Identify aspects of your situation that required you to do further investigation before you could proceed.
>
> Sum up what you think was the biggest stretch for you in taking on this change.

As you put yourself back in the moment when you were addressing this change in your life, take a few steps back from its successful conclusion. While examining the different ways that you moved from start to finish with your personal change, you may find that (1) some external input or resources were very valuable, but (2) you also had to draw on yourself and your personal commitment to this initiative in order to accomplish your goal. Look at the three examples below of the same personal challenge, and how differently each was handled.

Getting So Much Older

Annette: When my mother fell in the garage and broke her hip, it caught us by surprise. We had to make quick decisions. My brothers came from the east and west coasts, and we held a family council meeting while she was in the hospital. We had known that she was becoming less able to manage her life on her own, but were reluctant to intervene. We respected her repeated wish to "Let me do things on my own" even though we knew things would have to change. The doctors agreed with us, and we all presented a united front: It was time to move to assisted living. She was very angry, and we left her room many times so she wouldn't see how much she'd upset us. After the first month, we are still not sure that we made the right decision.

Resources Used: external events, consensus among family members in the face of strong emotion

Bradley: When my father fell in the garage and broke his hip, he used his cell phone to call me. I was out of the country, and so I had to call my brother who lived three hours away, in another state. We had the number of the neighbor, who assisted my father by arranging for, and going with my father to the hospital, via our local volunteer ambulance. We had worked out a chain of contacts and contingency plans with my dad a decade before and revisited these plans every Father's Day. As he went from the hospital to the rehabilitation center, we made the arrangements we had set up to move my youngest nephew (attending college nearby) into Dad's house. When he got home, we were ready. I realized, though, that we were almost on automatic pilot because we had planned everything out. We didn't let ourselves take time to acknowledge our feelings about his declining abilities.

Resources Used: external events, preexisting plans, including previously identified resources

Savona: When my mother fell in the garage and broke her hip, my sister and I were not talking to each other. We'd had so many disagreements about how we were handling Mother's aging that

(Continued)

෪ 67 ෪

(Continued)

we had given up even trying to understand each other's point of view. The emergency meant we had to drop our swords and find new ways to communicate. I think, in retrospect, that was the hardest part of coping with our mother's aging—learning to get along with each other. But as we did it (making use of the social workers in the hospital and the rehab facility), we became closer than we ever had before. We're not sure what will happen next for our mother, but have confidence that we will be able to discuss the options together.

Resources Used: external events, trained professionals

There is no single *right* way to plan for, or go through, a parent's aging process; what appears to be wise at one point in the process can be inhibiting later on. None of the approaches described above meets the needs of everyone involved. As you view the different resources used by each of the individuals above, you may become aware of how some of the approaches you use to handle challenging personal situations could become resources for you down the road.

In order to get maximum benefit out of the middle of this chapter, you'll be reconsidering the challenge you selected in 6.1 and make use of the next few challenges to dissect your own experience. As you do so, you can find within it things you did, or aspects of the situation, that you might be able to use in other settings.

Change Challenge 6.2	Recognizing the Skills That Made the Difference

Briefly describe skills you used to accomplish the change initiative you described in the previous challenge. Be as specific as you can about the skills you already had, as well as those you developed along the way.

How did you determine your goals and timelines? How did you test out your ideas in advance of, and during, your change initiative?

When things did not go according to plan, how did you make adjustments?
Who, if anyone, assisted you?

What emotional supports did you need to accommodate the changes in your approach?

Sum up what you think was the most valuable skill you used while making this change.

As you thought back over this accomplishment, you may have, for the first time, identified skills you developed or used. Perhaps you also gained new insights about the change effort you completed. Although you weren't aware of each of these skills consciously at the time, by standing back and looking at what you accomplished retrospectively, they may be in sharper focus now. Consider the description that follows.

Moving Made Me Bold

Married to a spouse whose career required relocations, I have moved 20 times, to a total of 12 states. After every move, I've found a teaching job within a few months of arrival. Every time, I had to go through the sequence of letting go, adjusting, and starting up again. I had to develop skills to discover how to fit into established situations, which included learning how to make new friends. Each time I joined the faculty of a school, I had to watch carefully how I was welcomed. I learned to be patient and not assume that everyone who greeted me warmly was ready to be a friend.

I've learned so much about myself in this process. My former shyness has given way to a curiosity about other people. Rather than being focused on myself, I've had to shift the center of my attention to others. What I've found is that as I got better and better at asking questions, I became less tentative. My questions sometimes led to interesting discussions, which on occasion translated into friendships. And another amazing outcome was that I became much more empathetic toward newcomers!

If I hadn't had to make so many adjustments, I doubt that I would have gained the ability to watch myself, give myself time to make mistakes, and learn from experience. But I know I can count on these skills now and adjust to other changes more easily as well.

—Olivia, physical education teacher

As this teacher became better at self-observation and alert to cues in her social environment, adjustments to new circumstances became easier. When systematically analyzing our life changes, we can learn a lot by itemizing what is working against us. Use the checklist in the Challenge below to reflect on your experiences:

Change Challenge 6.3 | Overcoming Obstacles

Consider the following types of obstacles that might have intruded on you during your accomplishment of your personal change initiative. Check all that you encountered. When you have done that, go back and select one to analyze more thoroughly, in order to examine how you prevented it from stopping you.

- ❏ Ran out of energy
- ❏ Ran out of time
- ❏ Changes in the availability or insights of the people involved required a different approach
- ❏ Something unexpected took place in other parts of my life, and I had to readjust my approach
- ❏ A resource upon which I was counting failed to materialize
- ❏ Expected outcomes didn't occur
- ❏ Other_____

(Continued)

(Continued)

Select one obstacle noted and describe how you overcame it:

_____

_____

_____

_____

_____

Ideally, reflecting on the skills you used, and the obstacles you overcame, sharpened your understanding of how you accomplished your change initiative in your personal life.

Change Challenge 6.4 | Generalizing

Match one of your upcoming change initiatives to something you learned in accomplishing your personal goal in Change Challenges 6.2 and 6.3. Consider the following prompts to enable you to make the translation from the personal to the professional:

When I think back on my personal changes, I am most proud that I was able to:

_____

_____

_____

When I imagine myself as a steady and capable teacher, I can envision using this aspect of my personal life to assist me:

_____

_____

_____

When I look at the skills that I have used to successfully handle a personal challenge, I anticipate that this one could really assist me in my professional setting:

_____

_____

_____

Being able to capitalize on this personal skill in my professional setting would make me proud:

_____

_____

_____

Take advantage of the things you have learned to do in your personal setting, so that you can make use of them in your professional setting. The following section of this chapter enables you to get started in the planning of a professional change initiative.

FOUR STEPS FOR STARTING A PROFESSIONAL CHANGE INITIATIVE

Picture an experienced competitive swimmer: the swimmer takes advantage of every opportunity to get an extra boost.

- The start: diving into the pool, and getting as far ahead of the other swimmers as possible.
- During the race: using the pool's sides as a resource for pushing off with extra energy at the end of each lap.
- Staying focused: paying attention to one's own rhythm and form to be successful.

The swimmer makes use of practice and of the adrenalin of the competition to try to win the race. These same strategies are relevant to teachers, as shown in the following example.

This is my mantra: "Patience, persistence, and have a clear idea of what you hope to accomplish." I had been searching for a way to bring my love of the Civil War beyond my fifth-grade class, into the school as a whole. When I heard Drew Gilpin Faust discuss her book about death and the Civil War,[1] I knew I had my entry point. She brought together emotions, personal narratives, history, and information about practices that are with us today (including dog tags and military burial).

I began with a book review at one of our PTA meetings, and that got us off to an amazing start. Parents who had never been part of our school's activities before got involved in showcasing local artifacts, and sharing the family stories from our community during the Civil War. Each step forward we took (assembling committees, involving students, connecting with the local historical society) required me to gather up my patience and continue to stay energized. Now, three years later, we have a schoolwide curriculum that involves members of the community, a Web site, and an annual cemetery project to honor our Civil War veterans. I had no idea how much work was involved, but I also wouldn't have imagined how satisfied I'd feel when it all came together.

—Nathan, Grade 5 teacher and history buff

As you think about your own commitment to turning one of your change initiatives into reality, follow the steps below to move from thought to action.

Step One: Identify Aspirations

Take time to consider what you regard as essential for a classroom to be a place of vitality and learning. This core of your vision for teaching is your starting point. Pickering (2006), after exploring the question of how teachers change, concluded that it is our core beliefs that determine our ability to make a change, because they shape our "sense of

---

[1] Faust, D. G. (2008). *This republic of suffering: Death and the American Civil War*. New York: Knopf.

what is possible, plausible and desirable" (p. 329). As a member of your school community, the design of change would likely begin where both Senge (1990) and Hall and Hord (2006) start out, with the development of a shared vision. The challenge in designing your own teaching environment is to verbalize your hopes for yourself, your students (and their families), your colleagues, and your school as a whole. Make use of the challenge below to envision the hopes you have for yourself.

Change Challenge 6.5 Looking for What Matters Most

Select *one or two questions* to record answers that you think are most relevant to your current classroom or school setting.

1. How do you stay motivated to teach? In what ways do your motivations appear in your classroom?

   _____
   _____
   _____

2. What aspects of your daily or weekly routine enable you to inspire yourself to reach beyond the things you *have* to do, to accomplish the things you *want* to do?

   _____
   _____
   _____

3. What have you seen your students accomplish that has invigorated you to pump more energy into your classroom?

   _____
   _____
   _____

4. How have you and your students benefited when you have established successful relationships with members of your students' families?

   _____
   _____
   _____

5. When you want to have an honest conversation with a colleague about what you hope to accomplish, to whom do you turn? What do you talk about?

   _____
   _____
   _____

6. Who among your colleagues is most likely to share your aspirations for your students and yourself?

   _____
   _____
   _____

7. Envision your school five years after you have left it. What would you like others to identify as your legacy?

   _____
   _____
   _____

Step Two: Inventory Resources

The design of your change initiative requires use of as many supports as you can provide for yourself, some of which may be newly apparent to you as a result of your reflection on your personal change experience. Supports may include a resource network (Cramer, 2006, p. 154) — a group of people who are outside your regular circle of professional contacts. By developing a broader circle of individuals, and sharing with them readings, and Web sites to use to explore your options for educational change, you are likely to expand conversations with your colleagues. This, in turn, can lead you to incorporate ideas that had not previously been a part of your initiative. One of the teacher participants in our research project highlighted the value of connecting with other teachers in this way: "Reaching out to those more experienced than myself has proven to be the most significant change. Calling upon their expertise, which can be done in a nonthreatening manner, has been critical to refining my craft."

Resource identification is the second step of the model that Adelman and Taylor (2007) designed to examine systemic change in schools. They suggest that in some cases existing resources might need to be used in ways that are relevant to the circumstances (e.g., "(re)deployed," p. 58) and are different from how they were used previously—"Resources that might be redeployed include those expended for nonproductive programs or ones that are addressing low priority needs" (p. 60). When looking at your own resources, you might identify intangibles (e.g., interests you have always wanted to pursue) as well as more predictable resources (like time and energy). The identification of resources is only the first step; the next is making use of the resources to adjust your mental model.

A mental model, much like an architect's preliminary drawings or a musician's composition notebook, is a starting point for any change initiative. It is the "blue sky thinking" that generally fits into the early stages of strategic planning or other big initiatives. However, it is only the beginning. Senge (1990) identified the transformation of "mental models" as one of the requirements for doing things in new ways. Many times, the way to adjust the mental model is by incorporating new resources.

For example, Alger (2007) considers the adjusted mental models used by student teachers who are introduced to a new way of teaching literature, through the lens of social justice (p. 628). This new perspective led to fresh insights. As one of the student teachers explained:

> The link between social justice and literacy is not a concept that I had any real notion of prior to taking this class. However, it is a crucial component of nearly all that will take place under a teacher in a classroom. Only in understanding this link can a teacher hope to address the issues that are involved here and contribute to positive social change through literacy in their classroom. (p. 628)

As you make use of the personal experiences and values you explored earlier in this chapter, consider ways to take advantage of resources that exist outside your school setting, via the following challenge.

Change Challenge 6.6 Gathering Resources

Imagine your professional resources for an upcoming change initiative as a pantry full of options for your use. The following prompts will enable you to make sure that you have what you need before embarking on a change initiative in your school. Consider people, books, curricula, professional

(Continued)

(Continued)

development activities, and your own personal experiences as potential resources for your change initiative, in each of the following categories:

Resources for creative thinking (e.g., long showers, doodling, early morning jog):

_____

_____

_____

Resources for encouraging my early efforts (e.g., my cheerleaders, an image of the students who most need the benefit this change will bring):

_____

_____

_____

Resources for maintaining mental balance during the change initiative (e.g., yoga, prayer, visits with friends who share my optimism and hope):

_____

_____

_____

Resources for learning new skills (e.g., the Teacher Center or the school's professional development library, a friend who is a tech wiz):

_____

_____

_____

Resources for maximizing my confidence (e.g., a list of previous accomplishments, a log to note progress):

_____

_____

_____

Resources for jump-starting my sense of humor (loved ones, pets, a favorite comic strip, a friend who always makes me laugh):

_____

_____

_____

As you design your change initiative, maximize your use of a *variety* of resources throughout the start-up period. It is easy, after the initial burst of insight and energy, to lose focus and give up on your effort. By building in strategic use of multiple resources, you can anticipate this possibility and avoid it.

Step Three: Link Aspirations and Resources

The opportunity to design a change initiative enables teachers to create a transformation that benefits students. For many of the teachers in our research project, students and their needs were often the impetus for change. One teacher spoke for many when she said the motivation to change comes "when you feel you are not giving your students what they need to be the best."

Sometimes the resources needed to get the change underway are readily available:

- "[I know I want to make a change] when alumni return to visit and tell me what prepared them and what didn't prepare them for college. I want to get out of the classroom and into the hallways and into other classrooms to talk to my colleagues."
- "[I know I want to make a change] when I learn about something that sounds better for my students. I attend the reunions at the teachers' college spring and fall and find their information inspirational and cutting edge."

Sometimes, though, accessing resources takes more deliberate effort. Creativity may be needed to put together resources sufficient to the task. These efforts are worth making in pursuit of our aspirations. As teachers, we are constantly evaluating our students' progress toward mastery of learning standards. This practice can be turned inward, when we treat our vision for teaching (Step One above) as the "standards" by which we evaluate ourselves. "Standards-based" self-assessment reminds us to continue to hold ourselves accountable for incorporating a change initiative into our work and moves us closer to achieving our vision for teaching. As shown in the following example, making the connection between vision and resources can be the key to carrying out a change initiative.

I had always wanted to experience my school as an intellectually vital place, where teachers who wanted to grapple with the challenges of our students' complex lives could stretch their minds. I wanted it to be the opposite of the teachers' lunchroom, where people seem to do nothing but complain. As I began my second decade of teaching, I decided it was time to see if I could move past the thinking, into the doing.

To turn things around, I started a new club within my school that would stimulate us to give up the mental ruts we were in and see things differently. I partnered with a few professors at our local college who came from departments that provided unusual perspectives on our students' circumstances. Every month, we invited either one of the professors or a member of a local community organization to meet with our club to help us analyze a problem we had identified in our school. Then, by ourselves, we used some of their ideas to craft an action plan for our school.

The first year, we decided to learn more about teen pregnancy and sexuality; we became more conscious of the work we needed to do with parents and our community as a whole. The word of mouth about our group spread, and even the people who had started out as most skeptical came around by the end of the year. We selected hunger as our topic for next year. We already have more suggestions than we can use for turning concerns and talk into supports for our students.

—Catherine, ninth-grade English teacher, urban high school

As the match between the initial vision and the local college took place, change took place. This connection can enable you to move beyond ideas to action.

Change Challenge 6.7	Braiding the Vision With the Resources to Start Your Change Initiative

Return to the previous two challenges, and connect one vision you have for yourself as a teacher with one or two resources you identified. Develop the best way to match these up, so that you have the resources you need at the outset of your change initiative.

_____

_____

_____

Step Four: Anticipate Obstacles

It is naive to imagine change initiatives without factoring in the forces that exist in opposition to your change initiative. As Hall and Hord (2006) highlighted in their examination of problem solving (p. 90), adapting Lewin's Force Field Analysis, there is value in looking simultaneously at forces working toward and against change. Consider what you know to be impediments while also identifying the ways you would be able to overcome them, by using your skills and resources to get started on your change initiative. Consider the following activity to identify possible obstacles.

Change Challenge 6.8	Foreseeing the Obstacles to Your Change Initiative

Review the list of obstacles that may get in the way of your professional situation. Check the one(s) that you will need to take into account as you begin your change initiative.

Personal
- ❏ Run out of energy
- ❏ Run out of time
- ❏ People on whom I am counting might not come through
- ❏ Something unexpected might take place in other parts of my life
- ❏ A resource upon which I am counting might fail to materialize (e.g.,_____)
- ❏ Other:

Professional
- ❏ Administrative support is missing
- ❏ Professional climate doesn't support my initiative
- ❏ Hostility from or among coworkers
- ❏ Student demands or problems (e.g., _____)
- ❏ Community difficulties
- ❏ Other:

Looking Ahead

The preparation for change in your professional life involves being alert to signals within yourself. There may be opportunities to improve things, for yourself and your students. If you are unsettled in your current situation, you are expending energy in maintaining the status quo that might be put to better use improving it. Self-directed change can result in intellectual stimulation and professional development and can be a powerful antidote to boredom and disappointment. Chapter 7 offers a step-by-step process for implementing the change you have been considering.

Teacher-Directed Change

Working Within the Classroom

I n Chapter 6, we explored the first part of the change process—developing a plan for change that capitalizes on self-knowledge and past success. The focus of this chapter is to help teachers bring an upcoming change initiative to fruition.

IMPLEMENTING, EVALUATING, AND CELEBRATING SELF-DIRECTED CHANGE

Although it may seem that little similarity exists between the ways teachers initiate voluntary and mandated change (see Chapter 3 for a discussion of these types of changes), there are fundamental similarities. Contrast the following two examples—a voluntary project initiative is described by one of the teachers who participated in our research study, followed by the description by Kilgallon, Maloney, and Lock (2008) of a published research project reporting involuntary changes.

I reactivated a defunct reading council by rallying teachers to come to a gathering prepared with novel professional development ideas—not only focused on themselves, but also involving families and students in our community. The first year, we had a single event, which we planned very carefully. The second year, we had one in fall and one in spring. Each year, we have seen progress.

As a result of slow and careful progress, we have a full year of programming scheduled for the upcoming year. Activities for families, students, as well as for teachers, center on the question "What is important?" These unique workshops feature presenters who are the authors of the writing/reading activities—everyone comes away with something positive in literacy. We have a father/son writing team who have worked together since the son was in third grade. The son is now a senior in high school and will be a great role model for all students.

—Katya, fourth-grade teacher, completing her 23rd year of teaching

The outcomes of this initiative are similar to those of the mandated change which Kilgallon, Maloney, and Lock (2008) discuss. Kilgallon et al. underscore how "teachers are acknowledged as being the key factor in the successful implementation of educational change" (p. 24). They found, in a study of 63 early-childhood teachers in metropolitan preschools in Australia, the factors most useful in coping with imposed changes were

> positive attitude towards imposed changes . . . and accepting educational change as part of their teaching role led them to be "willing to have a go." These teachers indicated that maintaining a positive focus on impending changes led them to be proactive in seeking information and becoming involved in the change process. (p. 25)

What do these two different discussions of teachers' change actions have in common? In both cases, teachers *take control of their attitudes and actions.* Successful teachers do not look ahead to a change (desired or required) as an obligation, full of unknowns. Instead, they organize their approaches to any kind of change; they proceed through a series of actions that enable them to move ahead progressively as they accomplish their goals. In this chapter, we'll consider how to advance change initiatives—whether desired or required. Ideally, teachers would make use of the four steps provided in Chapter 6 prior to the recommendations provided here.

Step One: Aim High But Start Small

Begin change realistically: Rather than jumping off a 15-foot-high diving board and hoping for the best, start out with the 4-foot springboard. Don't lose sight of the goal of mastering the high dive; just plan for success by proceeding in familiar, manageable steps. The energy put into setting out to accomplish change must be phased, so that initial activities ease us into the change process.

Consider the example of teachers who work together on a new lesson design, like the *Frankenstein* project described by Ferrero (2006). Teachers in two high schools followed the steps identified in the previous chapter, making use of their internal emotional and cognitive signals. They were displeased with how they were spending their teaching days; they were tired of "teaching to the test." Instead, they decided to identify the skills their students needed to learn and provide a schoolwide curricula that was based on themes for each grade that would be the focus during four points in the academic year. Instead of changing everything in their schools all at once, they analyzed their students' skills as well as their own interests, using structures such as "public forums . . . organized like town halls, and adults and students alike prepare for and participate in them, forming a community of learners pursuing focused inquiry" (p. 13). This "low dive" approach to changing the interaction pattern of teachers and students within the school set the stage for the more extensive change.

The development of the actual *Frankenstein* unit is an example of a high dive.

> This curricular framework requires teachers to introduce 10th grade students to the Enlightenment, Romanticism, and the Industrial Revolution, and to help students see the connections between those historical developments and the contemporary world. . . . Because the curriculum is so multifaceted and collaboratively developed, teachers can play to their own strengths and interests. (p. 13)

The teachers involved in the projects described by Ferrero had to develop new ways of thinking about themselves, their content specialties, and each other's areas of expertise. Teachers and students came to see the learning process differently—in terms of content and process. The sense of uncertainty and "being intimidated" (as one student within the school described her initial feelings, p. 13) eventually led to a new sense of curiosity and confidence, related to the curriculum and the approach used within the school. Consider the following Change Challenge as the start of your change initiative.

Change Challenge 7.1	Starting Your Change

Identify a change that you anticipate within the year or two—something that you believe is very likely to happen, but is not yet on your "to do" list. Consider it as you go through the steps below.

Getting ready and starting small:

1. Consider four questions to design the low dive for your change initiative:

   - *Ask yourself:* What can I accomplish easily?
   - *Ask another person who is familiar with the situation:* How can you help me get started with this initiative?
   - *Ask a mentor who has been an excellent resource in the past:* Which of my talents do you think I can use to help myself get this project underway?
   - *Ask a recipient of the change effort:* How can you help me get this initiative started?

2. Select two of these questions and answer them briefly.

3. Line up three supports for yourself (motivational, logistical, informational) that will boost your confidence.

4. Plan for a debriefing process (journaling, discussion with a colleague, charting data) that will enable you to look at your overall goal and evaluate whether or not you have gotten the information you need to get the initiative underway when you are ready to do so.

Keeping your eye on the prize and aiming high:

1. Develop a step-by-step sequence of objectives that will enable you to accomplish your "high dive" goal. Make each step approximately equal in level of difficulty. Space your steps out in a time frame that is reasonable for you (e.g., one every two weeks or so).

2. Connect each step to two resources that you have found to be useful to you in the past. The resources can be people, places, books, ways of working—giving you the necessary support you can use at each step of the way.

3. Identify a change motivator that will enable you to initiate your change and address each of your objectives. This might focus on what you want to accomplish for yourself, for your students, for others in your school, or for your community. Keep that motivator in the forefront of your mind as you move through your initiative.

Step Two: Build a Timeline

Establishing timelines becomes automatic for teachers. Your class runs smoothly because of the way you have designed and integrated the curriculum, activities, and homework assignments. When you are out of your curricular "comfort zone," facing a project involving change, however, it is inevitable that any timeline you develop (with an objective for every two weeks or so, as suggested in Change Challenge 7.1, or a more compressed schedule) will need adjustment. In part, this is a function of the many other concurrent responsibilities you have when undertaking a change initiative—teachers rarely can carve out a specific period of time to dedicate to a single project. To address this problem, Reeves (2006) explains that "some school principals have a simple rule—they will introduce no new program until they remove at least one or two existing activities, plans, units or other time-consumers" (p. 89). Consider this idea in undertaking your new initiative, as you design a timeline that enables you to maintain momentum in spite of conflicting obligations.

Take advantage of what you have learned in setting out timelines for curriculum planning: plan forward toward a goal, or backwards from an end date. Either way, you will need to design not only your target dates, but ways to continue (and adjust) in spite of setbacks.

How do you make adjustments? Here are some practical options:

- Eliminate (or redesign) a portion of the overall project
- Lengthen your timeline
- Enlist additional resources

When you must make these adjustments, maintain your momentum. Although the adjustment seems in some ways to be a practical matter, usually emotions are involved.

Emotions are often linked to educational change—as alarms (letting us know to be on the alert) or doorbells (opening the door to a new opportunity). As teachers learn to seek out and use emotions as key indicators (e.g., something important is happening), they cease to be victims of their powerful emotions. Instead, they can become proactive, rather than reactive, and pursue new ways to work. Using emotions as resources enables teachers involved in change to continue to *control their initiatives*, rather than letting the *emotions (or the initiatives) control them*. Remaining alert to the strong emotions (either positive or negative) associated with teaching becomes the signal to open the door to educational change:

> Good teaching is charged with positive emotion. It is not just a matter of knowing one's subject, being efficient, having the correct competences, or learning all the right techniques. Good teachers are not just well-oiled machines. They are emotional, passionate beings who connect with their students and fill their work and their classes with pleasure, creativity, challenge and joy. (Hargreaves, 1998, p. 835)

Hargreaves's description of the work teachers do in their classrooms highlights aspects of a change initiative that is illustrated in the example below:

When it became clear that the standards movement was here to stay, I became an advocate within our social studies department for a common curriculum and common assessments, so that all teachers would cover the same content. This seemed like a logical plan, and I worked with a group of three teachers over the summer to draft key student learning outcomes (tied to our state standards) that were spaced throughout the year. We thought we had all our bases covered. We were excited about our opportunities for stimulating both student learning and parent involvement.

However, by October, it was clear that we had overestimated what was possible. We had one teacher who took an unexpected extended medical leave, another who was called up to serve in the National Guard, and a third who fought us over every idea we had proposed. We knew we had to regroup. We consciously fought our discouragement about not meeting our original timelines and our goals. We felt like we were on an emotional roller coaster, going from the high of September to the low of November. Just as all the leaves were falling off the trees, we felt like we were falling too. But in fact we had prepared emotionally as well as logistically in the planning stages, when we anticipated problems, so we didn't let our feelings of disappointment deter us from continuing.

After conversations with others in our district who had launched similar initiatives, we went back to the drawing board. We made major changes, not only scaling back on *what* we hoped to accomplish (spreading out the goals for the fall throughout the year) but *who* was involved. We decided to treat our start-up year as a pilot and only involve 25% of the classes in our effort. This included our planning group as well as a number of other teachers who had been eager to try out our ideas. The year ended with a daylong retreat about improvement in our students' performance, what we had accomplished as well as ideas about adjustments for the schoolwide implementation of the project the following year.

—Jaime, 18-year veteran social studies teacher and
member of the National Guard

As you design your timeline, remember to build in contingency time so that you can make the necessary adjustments. Be honest with yourself regarding progress early on, so that you can do what is needed to accomplish your goal (even in a modified form).

Step Three: Monitor Both Progress and Outlook

Developing routines for looking *back* at what has been accomplished and *ahead* to what remains to be done is essential. Much like working with a student who has not learned via traditional instructional strategies, building in methods for assessment and goal setting can smooth the progress of change initiatives. Pedro (2005) explained that preservice teachers who made use of either "verbal" or "written" reflections found that "reflections . . . came through their ability to link concepts to themselves, and to other significant individuals. Thus, they linked their reflections to their personal values" (p. 62). Instead of focusing only on the external measurements (e.g., the assessments they built in to determine if their students were making progress), teachers evaluated how well they were achieving their accomplishment of the equally important advancement of their personal values and beliefs.

The continuous process of reconsidering progress enables teachers to avoid overfocusing on what went wrong, and instead to give themselves credit for what went well. Identifying both what needs to be *continued,* as well as what needs to be *changed,* becomes the basis of identifying progress accurately.

True measurement of progress involves not only checking on the accomplishment of objectives, but also our outlook. Sagging outlooks pull us all down. Do the words of Reeves (2006) ring true for you?

Educators are drowning under the weight of initiative fatigue—attempting to use the same amount of time, money, and emotional energy to accomplish more and more objectives. That strategy, fueled by various mixtures of adrenaline, enthusiasm, and intimidation, might work in the short term. But eventually, each initiative added to the pile creates a dramatic decline in . . . effectiveness. (p. 89)

Teachers can determine whether they are buoyed up, or weighted down, by the initiative they have undertaken. Consider using the following questions to gauge your progress and your outlook:

Change Challenge 7.2 Staying Focused While Facing Fears

As with any change initiative, there is a tendency to focus on what is not going well and what remains to be accomplished. In this challenge, consider the things that might stand out for you in terms of the initiative you anticipate undertaking.

What do you know about *yourself* that will give you concerns about your progress on your initiative?

What do you know about the *context* (others in your school, your community) that will give you concerns?

What do you fear the accomplishment of your initiative will unleash (the Pandora's Box problem)?

What is the biggest thing that you feel stands in the way of the success of your initiative?

What accomplishments have you achieved that can assist you in planning ahead for the future?

As you design your method for assessing progress, address these concerns to anticipate them, and proactively prevent them from derailing your initiative.

In their interesting article contrasting focus on performance with concern about the affective aspects of teaching and learning, McNess, Broadfoot, and Osborn (2003) studied teachers in several countries to see how they face the increasing number of professional demands. They found that teachers meet their professional obligations in different ways:

While some teachers felt deskilled and restricted in their professional autonomy, there were others who had seized the potential for a margin of maneuver between the imposed centralized policies and their implementation . . . "creative mediation," while others had found ways of working within the guidelines and gained a new professional discourse, including new professional practices, in the process (Woods & Jeffrey, 1997). (p. 248)

The way we respond to mandated changes, or those we initiate, can vary not only by person, but also throughout the change initiative—at times we can feel hemmed in, while at other times, we can find new insights about our work and our options. (See Chapter 5 for a discussion of predictable variation within change initiatives.) We encourage you to avoid feeling trapped within your change initiative; instead, tap into creativity as a method for addressing unsatisfactory situations.

Step Four: Celebrate Small Victories

Yes! Stop and take pleasure in completing even the small steps that will eventually lead to the accomplishment of your goal. Even when there is more to be done, the time invested in savoring what has been achieved can help you move forward with greater satisfaction. Consider the advice of Masci, Cuddapah, and Pajak (2008), who examined different ways to assist a school in addressing mandated change and encouraged this activity: "Frequently celebrate successes . . . such celebration validates individual and group efforts and contributes to a stable, trusting, enjoyable environment that is arguably more productive . . . [A] dose of realism was also important: not all efforts were successful" (p. 66). The last sentence reminds us to be on guard against celebration for celebration's sake: not every accomplishment merits acknowledgement. However, consider some simple options, such as the following, to avoid overfocus on what remains to be done or adjusted, either on your own or while working with others:

- Include "good news" within your personal reflections on the week or at meetings.
- Select an "accomplishment of the week" to highlight when reviewing weekly plans.
- Grant yourself, and others involved in the change initiative, legitimate mental "vacations" from the work after reaching an important milestone, or after a certain amount of time has passed.
- Plan and participate in a social celebration: happy hour, ice cream "spectacular," informal potluck meal.
- Design certificates to mark accomplishment of parts of the initiative.
- Sponsor a surprise breakfast.
- Seek out and share nonfood surprises, including flowers, notes, motivational Web sites.
- Share notes received from others who have noticed the change initiative.

The essential aspect of celebration is to genuinely give ourselves credit for something that we have done that advances our change agenda. We shouldn't think of this as an "extra" or "special treat" but rather as a part of our regular diet. Maintaining a healthy outlook on change requires regular celebrations as progress happens, rather than only at the end.

In the winter of my third year of teaching, our school adopted a new assessment plan. We were given just a few months to work with specialists in our state and were expected to have something ready to pilot by June. Many of us felt angry about the unrealistic timeline. It was challenging to stay invested in the effort, with all the other work we still had to do.

What helped was a biweekly treasure hunt for "What Went Right." We formed teams and tallied up the accomplishments our team had achieved (after we interviewed each other and looked at our work products). Some of our achievements were so small that we probably would have ignored them were it not for this competition. We'd bring a description of what we found to our Friday gathering in the school library and then vote for our favorites—most unexpected, most inspiring, most

(Continued)

(Continued)

likely to advance us toward our goal. We'd end our time together with popsicles, chattering informally about the accomplishments we'd discovered. Sometimes we adjourned for a Happy Hour.

What amazed me about this process—I was one of the skeptics at the start—was how it brought us together. It enabled us to keep a look out for what we were actually accomplishing. By the time we got to the implementation of our pilot, we were prepared. We knew that we would be both proud of and discouraged by our results and were well prepared to examine everything.

—Yonge, eighth-year English teacher in an urban charter middle school

Step Five: Shift Strategies to Make Adjustments

It is inevitable that, no matter how experienced the planner or how ideal the circumstances, adjustments will have to be made. Sometimes all that is needed are simple midcourse corrections, accommodations to logistical potholes. Other times, however, there are more complex problems to address. The change process can bring to the surface unresolved issues; resources we counted on vanish; people who once seemed to be eager participants turn out to be little more than bystanders; our own energy and enthusiasm for the project may sag. Before we let our project drift away, it's helpful to consider that, as Marshak (1996) explains,

Change does involve *loss* as well as gain. . . . In considering the nature of loss, we need to remember that the extent of any particular loss, its power and value, lies not in any objective measure but in the eyes and heart of the person who is experiencing the losing. . . . [T]o the teacher experiencing the loss, it may involve his or her core sense of worth. Loss can threaten our self-concept and self-esteem. (p. 75)

As we teach ourselves to look candidly at our change initiative, it is like looking in the mirror. Instead of looking objectively at the task at hand, we see ourselves—sometimes in a mirror that distorts. Why is that? Marshak theorizes that when we have trouble, or are unable to make progress, we are actually caught up in some personal struggles:

I believe that a great deal of what we see as educators' resistance to change is a manifestation of grief in the face of actual or expected losses. Many of the attitudes and behaviors that "stuck" educators manifest can be more fully understood if we see them as unsuccessful grieving. (p. 76)

As teachers, we need to reframe the inevitable challenges we will face during change initiatives anew and instead see them as opportunities to revisit what we are doing. Rather than imagining them as the bandits, come to steal our good ideas away, we need to see them as someone at the door with an unexpected package—only we can decide what is inside the box. When you face this moment, do the following: Bring together

(1) your recollection of the initial aspirations you and others in your group had at the outset,

(2) your internal reflections about your own reactions and those of your colleagues to what has happened thus far, and

(3) a reconsideration of the strategies you are using to accomplish your goals.

These three activities can enable you to make that package at the door a gift rather than an unwanted, unnecessary distraction and lead you to making the necessary adjustments. We move past the traps that prevented us from seeing our situation without distortion and free ourselves to adjust. As Einstein said, "Insanity is doing the same thing over and over again and expecting different results." When we are frustrated or discouraged, it is time to take a step back and consider our options.

One helpful approach is to develop a list of relevant questions, to enable us to get perspective on our effort. The following examples, developed by Marshak (1996), illustrate ways to get perspective on a change initiative, which can lead to adjusting our approach:

- What will we as an institution gain from this innovation? What will I as an individual gain from this innovation? What are my feelings about these gains?
- What will we as a school lose from this innovation? How do I feel about these losses? What will I as an individual lose from this innovation? How do I feel about these losses?
- Are we ready to move ahead with this innovation now, given all that we know about its value, and about both what we are gaining and losing, and how we feel about this? (p. 76, 77)

Selecting and using relevant questions can give us a new perspective. These questions can help us to anticipate that we will need to fine-tune our approach. The plan you developed for your change initiative is a starting point, but it is likely to need adjustment.

One of the teachers who participated in our research study noted that an attitude modification transformed her outlook and her approach: "I found out I cannot change the world. I honestly thought I could during my first year of teaching. I woke up and realized I must focus on the things I can change. It was liberating." This insight enabled the teacher to reinvest in her teaching in a new way.

Instead of getting discouraged about the need to make adjustments, teach yourself to anticipate this inevitable action as merely "tweaking" your change initiatives. Give yourself permission to experience the discouragement of the setback. Develop the habit of looking at such attitude modifications as routine rather than as exceptions. This enables us to view plans not as contracts, but rather as works in progress. When plans are no longer viewed as fixed, they are more likely to remain in use. As teachers, we adjust our lesson plans automatically and maintain our optimism based on small successes experienced by our students. We can learn to do the same thing with our change initiatives.

Step Six: Sustain Commitment

The success of your change initiative depends on your ability to bring together your intellect, your emotions, and your stamina as prerequisite to professional change.

Educational change initiatives do not just affect teachers' knowledge, skill, and problem-solving capacity. They affect a whole web of significant and meaningful relationships that make up the work of schools and that are at the very heart of the teaching and learning process. Educational change efforts affect teachers' relationships with their students, the parents of those students, and each other. Teachers make heavy emotional investments in these relationships. Their sense of success and satisfaction depends on them. (Hargreaves, 1998, p. 838)

Make use of the following challenge to protect the personal investment you have made in undertaking a change effort:

Change Challenge 7.3	Sustaining Commitment

Make a commitment to yourself to stick with a change project that is underway. Recognize the challenges you are facing. Give yourself the pep talk you need to keep on going:

At the start, I was worried I would be able to:

Now that I have been working at it, I am proud that I am now able to:

When I face difficulties, I am tempted to give up because:

Instead, I want to remind myself that I have the ability to keep going, and to:

Looking Ahead

Though it may look like magic and mystery, bringing about change is a matter of making a systematic and sustained effort to achieve something worthwhile. We are motivated to undertake the effort, perhaps despite misgivings, because we believe that ultimately it will help students. In Part IV of *A Teacher's Guide to Change,* our focus broadens from making changes in our own classrooms and schools to benefit our own students, to working for change more broadly.

Part IV

Leading Change

Part IV of *A Teacher's Guide to Change* illustrates how teachers who have learned to make changes in their teaching can view themselves as people who can, and sometimes should, assume the role of change agents. We show that the skills needed for leading change are closely related to skills good teachers use every day in their classrooms. In Chapter 8, we examine a variety of circumstances in which classroom teaching skills are used in the broader contexts of school and community. In Chapter 9, we explore the specific skills teachers can use to lead change among their colleagues.

CHAPTER 8

Teacher-Led Change

Expanding Beyond the Classroom

Teachers who lead change probably are a lot like you. They are teachers first and foremost, with little interest in high-profile leadership roles. But they find themselves in situations where leadership is needed to bring about an important change, and they step up to the plate. They are not seeking "to escape their classrooms, but to create more options within their classrooms" (Rallis & Rossman, 1995, p. 117). Most of the time, they become involved in a change effort in order to influence policies and practices that impact their own students. Often, however, they end up making a difference in the lives of children they will never meet. The account that follows describes how a first-grade teacher named Hannah became a leader of change without ever intending to do so.

For me, the watershed moment occurred when our superintendent mandated standardized testing for all students, including those in our K–2 school. I was an experienced early childhood educator, and I was confident in my judgment about developmentally appropriate practice—and I knew it didn't include having first graders bubble in answer sheets. I worried that we would take a giant step backward if we became focused on the kinds of skills that can be measured by pencil and paper tests for primary grade students.

I'm a naturally reserved person. I don't like to stand out in a crowd, and I really don't like conflict. So I hesitated when parents of students in my class asked me to join them at a school board meeting to protest the new policy. I told them I'd think about it.

Gradually I realized that I had to join them—and in fact, that we teachers should be out front on this. But I dreaded it. So I asked a friend on the faculty to join me. He agreed and together we brought it up at a grade-level meeting. Someone suggested we write a letter to our principal

(Continued)

(Continued)

outlining our reasons, thinking maybe she could use it if she needed ammunition in an administrative team meeting. I'm a decent writer, so they asked me to do the first draft. I went to the Web site of a professional organization for early childhood educators to get research to back up our points, and what I found there helped to strengthen my resolve.

I ended up speaking at the school board meeting, with my voice quavering the whole time. We revised our letter to the principal and published it in the local paper. As a result of that, I was asked to attend a series of Saturday morning meetings of people in the community who wanted to influence the direction of the school board. I recommended that we ask a former board member to run again, and when she agreed, I helped write her campaign brochure.

Eventually we were able to get some change in the new testing policy. The requirements were scaled back to begin standardized testing in the middle of third grade. We'd have preferred to leave it where it had been before, at the end of fourth grade, but that was the best we could get.

While it was going on, the experience was stressful. But it helped me see that I can help lead an effort to make a change, and that I can bring other people along in that effort. I didn't know that about myself.

—Hannah, veteran teacher of grades K–4, member
of National Association for the Education of Young Children (NAEYC)

Hannah might not call herself a leader, but Christopher Lowney would. In *Heroic Leadership*, Lowney (2003) argues that the prevailing view of leaders—as take-charge people whose decisions at critical junctures lead directly to results—is actually a cultural stereotype that fails to capture the essence of leadership. Using examples of the leadership qualities evident in the 16th century priests who founded the religious order popularly known as the Jesuits, Lowney shows that leadership is not as much about defining moments and grand results as it is about taking ordinary opportunities to make subtle, consistent differences, by motivating ourselves to act on our values and convictions. Urging us to recognize that we are all leaders, all of the time, Lowney asks the following questions:

> If the general rallying hundreds of troops for a decisive engagement is a leader, aren't the parents who molded these same troops into conscientious, self-confident adults leaders as well? If the manager navigating colleagues through a work crisis is a leader, isn't the person who encourages a friend to tackle a difficult personal problem also a leader? If the president nurturing the company's future managers is a leader, aren't they also leaders who years earlier taught these same rising corporate stars to read and write and think? (p. 17)

Lowney maintains that effective leaders "make themselves and others comfortable in a changing world" (p. 29) because, while they are flexible and open to new ideas, they are firmly grounded in their principles and values. In the account that opened this chapter, we see that Hannah was persuaded to take on a leadership role when she saw a threat to the principles of early childhood education that she valued.

CHARACTERISTICS OF CHANGE LEADERS

In many ways, teachers who lead change are like Hannah and like most dedicated teachers:

- They enter teaching motivated by a desire to make a difference in children's lives, and they experience stress when conditions limit their ability to do so (McLaughlin, Pfeifer, Swanson-Owens, & Yee, 1986).
- They are careful listeners, sensitive to the needs and concerns of others.
- They are good collaborators, engaging the support and energies of other people, because important change is seldom within the power of any one person to create.
- They take on new roles because they perceive a need for change. While they may look back on their involvement in change initiatives as stimulating and gratifying, personal satisfaction is not often the motivating factor in their decision to become involved.
- They move beyond their comfort zones, as Hannah did, because that's what is needed to get the job done.

However, Hannah's experience is different from that of most teachers who responded to our survey in one important respect. Hannah worked to reverse an impending change that she feared would be harmful; the teacher leaders in our study usually worked to establish something positive rather than to prevent something negative. They sought to improve existing programs and to develop ways to respond to unmet needs. Although it may be true that there is a small group of teachers who experience teaching as "a continuous uphill struggle requiring the expenditure of considerable professional energies just to stop bad things from happening" (Gregory & Smith, 1987, p. 21), the teachers we studied were not among them. They were thoughtful, committed, and decidedly proactive.

Two of every three teachers we surveyed (67%) reported that they had initiated change that had an impact beyond their classrooms. These change initiators were not former or future administrators: Only 3% reported holding a previous leadership position, such as assistant principal or preschool administrator, and only 6%, indicated that they planned to pursue an administrative position in the next five years. While 36% of our respondents indicated that they had taken on peer leadership roles that were recognized as such by their districts, usually as team leaders or department chairs, the most common form of leadership was informal. For example, 71% reported that they had served as mentors to new or struggling teachers.

Sometimes teachers are not the ones to initiate change, but they end up with leading roles nonetheless. One teacher in our study was asked to pilot a new inclusive education class, another to review the research on homework policies and make recommendations to the site-based team, still another to represent the school on a committee of community agencies developing a school-to-work program. Hall and Hord (2001) might call these teachers *consigliore*—people who are indispensable partners to change initiators and leaders.

SPHERES OF INFLUENCE

Teachers who lead change expand their influence beyond their classrooms. Danielson (2006) reports that teacher leaders typically concentrate their efforts

Figure 8.1 Teachers' Spheres of Influence

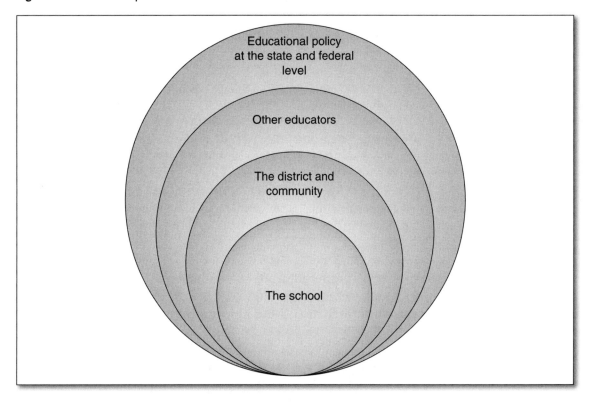

within their schools and districts, and this was the case with most teachers in our study. Some, however, reported change initiatives directed at the broader community outside the school district, either within their professional organizations or at the teaching profession as a whole. In this chapter, we will use their words and examples to illustrate how teachers bring about change in the schoolwide curriculum and in cocurricular offerings; reach out to families and the community; strengthen the profession by leading professional development programs for other teachers; and work at the state and national levels to shape policies that can transform teaching and learning.

Curriculum Development

No one works more closely with student learning, so taking the lead in curriculum change is natural for teachers. Consider these examples:

> My previous school held a Colonial Day for all of the fourth grades each year, and I got one started when I came here. It was the first time the school had done something that got the whole grade involved in a single project.
>
> —Ayda, fourth-grade teacher

I got our math department to agree to make a proposal to the administration that we extend our one-year algebra course into two years. We don't have a department chair, so I had to be the point person. Even though the current Board of Education is emphasizing raising standards, they could see our logic and approved the proposal.

—Ron, ninth- and tenth-grade mathematics teacher

I proposed, got approval for, and began teaching a new course in forensic science. It's a popular course that helps our science department reach out to kids who don't see themselves as science students. The superintendent has asked me to visit the other middle school in our district to encourage them to do something similar.

—Lauren, seventh-grade science teacher

At the state conference for special ed. teachers I became aware that all the emphasis on getting students with disabilities to pass state tests had led to less time for things that aren't tested, like occupational skills. I volunteered to work on the state committee that recommended revisions to the career prep standards for students with disabilities.

—Rolando, high school resource teacher

Through their curriculum development work, the teachers quoted above had an influence that extended beyond their classrooms. Their efforts show teachers leading change in different arenas:

Within their grade levels or subject areas, teachers use their knowledge of students and content to make minor changes, such as

- recommending adjustments to a newly adopted curriculum, and
- establishing common final exams so all students have the opportunity to learn the standard curriculum.

Across their schools or districts, teachers undertake larger efforts, involving other grade levels and school buildings and requiring more time and energy, such as

- embarking on interdisciplinary projects that bring colleagues together in new ways, and
- advocating for new models for curriculum and instruction, for example, the Responsive Classroom approach to teaching.

Beyond their local communities, at the state and national level, teachers band together to work for change, often through their professional organizations, for example by

- serving on review panels for state assessments, such as New York's Regents Exams, or
- seeking appointment to committees revising the learning standards of the discipline, for example, through organizations like the National Council for the Social Studies, or the Professional Standards Committee of the Council for Exceptional Children.

Needs Survey, Part 1   Focus on Curriculum Development

Consider the major components of your curriculum. These can be within a content area you know in depth or across a range of subjects. Don't overlook areas such as civics, fine and performing arts, or family and career sciences, and skills such as critical thinking, character education, or social development.

What weaknesses exist in your curriculum?

_____

_____

_____

Which of these can be strengthened through action at the local level?

_____

_____

_____

What steps can you take to initiate or advance efforts to strengthen the curriculum?

_____

_____

_____

With whom (inside and outside your school and community) can you partner to ensure that these steps lead to change?

_____

_____

_____

What problems do you anticipate in moving these changes along?

_____

_____

_____

Cocurricular and Extracurricular Programming

The teachers in our study also reported initiating and leading change in cocurricular programming for students. Some of their efforts were intended to *strengthen students' academic skills:* (1) setting up an after-school cross-age tutoring program for at-risk students, (2) reestablishing the school newspaper, and (3) starting a math club focused on playing games to reinforce math skills. Other teachers wanted to *provide a richer experience for students in specific content areas.* For example, a high school music teacher resurrected the forgotten tradition of the school drama production and a middle school English teacher started a literary magazine featuring the work of students and teachers. Some change efforts aimed to *address the needs of students whom teachers identified as underserved.* One teacher brought the Science Olympiad to her school, and another established the first Odyssey of the Mind chapter in his district.

I set up a mentoring program, pairing at-risk students with teachers who agree to take a special interest in them. We all get together for things like group lunches, after-school roller-skating parties, and trips to local attractions. Getting that project off the ground, and knowing that it has been good for teachers as well as students, was one of the things that led me to think about applying for National Board certification. I wrote one of my entries about the mentoring project.

—Corinne, special education partner
in a cotaught sixth-grade inclusion class

I worked very hard to get a peer mediation/conflict resolution program going in our school. I brought in professionals from the community to help us get started, then the school social worker and I took over, and gradually I faded out. It feels good to see something I started still going on, when so many things in education fall by the wayside when the main proponents are no longer involved.

—Rashima, fourth-grade teacher

Through personal contacts, I started an exchange program with a Scottish school. I left the district eight years ago, but the program is still going strong, with about 20 students from Scotland coming here and 20 of our students going there each year.

—Richard, former high school English teacher

Some teachers became involved in leading change efforts because they wanted to *improve the social climate of the school,* often to *create a more welcoming environment* for students who might otherwise be on the margins. Such projects were often near and dear to the teachers' hearts, and they invested a great deal of themselves in change efforts. One teacher who grew up with an older brother with multiple disabilities described her cautious efforts to bring the World of Difference program to her school, and her pride in seeing it spread to other schools in the district. Another, the father of a gay son, shared the frustration and regret he felt when he was unable to gain support for the establishment of a Gay-Straight Alliance at his school.

Needs Survey, Part 2	Focus on Cocurricular and Extracurricular Activities for Student Development

Consider the students you teach, not just as students, but as future parents, voters, employees and employers—as active and engaged members of your community.

Which students are relatively underserved in your school?

_____

_____

_____

(Continued)

(Continued)

Which students are "invisible" to their peers?

_____

_____

_____

What are the most pressing needs among the students in your school?

_____

_____

_____

How can you harness the incredible energy of students to help meet the needs of some of the underserved students in your school?

_____

_____

_____

What values cannot be developed well through the standard curriculum?

_____

_____

_____

If your school added an extra half-hour to each day, for extracurricular options, what would be the best way for students to spend it?

_____

_____

_____

What gives you pleasure in your life outside of school that you would like to share with students?

_____

_____

_____

Outreach to Families and the Community

From the times of one-room schoolhouses, teachers have recognized the importance of building a community of learners within their classrooms. Teachers who lead change know that the community of learners must extend beyond their classrooms, because learning must extend beyond the school walls and the traditional school day. They reach out to families, of course, but they also seek opportunities to *build support for education* in the wider community. Rallis and Rossman (1995) describe these teachers as bridge builders and credit them with blurring boundaries *to enlarge our sense of community.*

Following the lead of a teacher from another district (and with his help) I started a club called STAR—Students Taking Action and Responsibility. The students do community service projects, like raising money for the local shelter for the homeless and collecting pet food to leave at the food pantry for people who can't afford to purchase it themselves.

—Kevin, fifth-grade teacher

As both a sister of an individual with special needs and a teacher, I saw the need for family members of individuals with special needs to get together. I sent out flyers and began to organize a districtwide parent support group for parents of students in special education. Though my building principal and a few others supported the idea, the director of special education did not, so I had to back off. But the group liked the idea so much, they picked up the ball and ran with it on their own.

—Maria, fourth-grade teacher and sister
of Stacy, a 43-year-old woman with cerebral palsy

The examples reflect the desire to *respond to the needs of people under stress* that prompts some teachers to seek ways to provide emotional and financial support. One group of teachers hosted a community dinner to raise funds for the unexpected expenses of a family with a parent serving in the military overseas; it had the added benefit of demonstrating the school's support for military families in the area. To help single parents of children with disabilities, two teachers developed a respite care program, training high school students as caregivers for children with mild disabilities. Teachers can also be the catalysts for communities to come together to help others in distress. Schools in a community in Texas that had experienced a natural disaster sent members to New Orleans to assist them in planting trees, so that they would have birds returning to their area the following spring.

Teachers also lead change when *they help families and community members understand new curricular initiatives.* Sometimes a school adopts a proven program; Everyday Math, Project Lead the Way, the Responsive Classroom and the International Baccalaureate program are good examples cited by our survey respondents. Other times the new approach is not so much adopted as adapted and tailored to fit the school; our respondents mentioned portfolio assessments, project-based learning, conflict resolution and service learning programs in this regard. Whatever the program, its success depends in part on the extent to which it is accepted by families and other community members. The likelihood that the programs will gain the necessary support will be increased if teachers take the initiative to introduce them to the community. Like the teachers in our study, they may (1) use evening workshops to explain the purposes and processes of new programs, (2) create informal opportunities to share the reasons they endorse a change and to listen to community members' concerns about it, or (3) develop and distribute materials illustrating how parents can help their children make the transition to a new way of doing things.

Teachers are uniquely qualified *to build support for education in the community.* Teachers' unions can be the vehicle for change initiatives. To counter a perception among some segments of the community that union attention focuses narrowly on teachers' self-interests, one teacher convinced her union to sponsor annual displays at the local mall to show the scope of the curriculum and to highlight students' achievements. Another used her position as an officer in the union to lead the establishment of union-supported college scholarships. Her school district is small, in an economically depressed rural area with a low rate of post-secondary education. The new scholarships are funded through student-teacher volleyball and basketball games that have become bright spots in the long winters of their northeastern community.

Needs Survey, Part 3	Focus on Families and Community

What are two or three compelling needs of families of students with whom you have worked?

_____

_____

_____

What structures exist in your school that can be called on to address those needs?

_____

_____

_____

What misperceptions about education exist in your community?

_____

_____

_____

How can you use your skills as a teacher to help people develop a more accurate understanding of your school's mission and practices?

_____

_____

_____

In what segments of the community is there a need to build greater support for education?

_____

_____

_____

How can you enlist the assistance of your colleagues to reach out to those segments?

_____

_____

_____

Professional Development for Teachers

Teachers can be tough customers when it comes to professional development. If we are absent from the classroom for a day, we know that, even with the best substitute teachers, our students will experience some loss of learning. So we want professional development activities that outweigh this cost—activities that are practical and have direct relevance for our classrooms. That's why other teachers are often the best ones to *plan and deliver professional development activities.*

> I investigated the Wilson Reading program, and asked the district to send me for summer training. I now help other teachers learn to use it.
>
> —Angela, sixth-grade special education teacher
>
> Because of the experiences I have had not only as a veteran science teacher, but as the parent of two children with autism, I have begun to speak to teachers and college students about how best to address the needs of the increasing population of children with autism, to make it possible for them to succeed in the general education classroom.
>
> —Suzanna, seventh- and eighth-grade science teacher

Teachers skilled in new approaches to teaching may be eager to spread the word about what they have found. They use faculty meetings and superintendent's conference days to convince their colleagues of the value of the new approach and help them begin to use it. To extend their reach, some take advantage of "train the trainer"programs and earn credentials that enable them to offer professional development to teachers in other areas.

Another example of teacher-led change is the introduction to U.S. schools of *lesson study*, a professional development program regularly used in Japan that is gaining popularity in the U.S. (Lewis, Perry, Hurd, & O'Connell, 2006). Groups of teachers plan a lesson together and choose one person to teach it while the others observe and take notes. Later, the person who served as instructor leads a discussion to analyze the lesson and make changes to the plan, which can then be used by other teachers. The emphasis is on the structure and outcomes of the lesson plan, which was jointly developed, rather than on the performance of the instructor. Lesson study is a means for teachers to lead each other in a collaborative effort to change instructional practices.

Needs Survey, Part 4   Focus on Professional Development

Consider the hundreds of skills you call on each day as a teacher—skills in instruction and classroom management, in promoting cognitive development, in creating a climate that encourages holistic development, in engaging families in their children's education.

(Continued)

(Continued)

What are your particular strengths as a teacher? (Hint: For what do parents and students thank you, supervisors commend you, colleagues ask you?)

_____

_____

_____

Which of your strengths represents an area of weakness—and therefore an opportunity for growth—for other teachers?

_____

_____

_____

Recall the professional development activities that you have found beneficial.

- What did they have in common?
- Which of these features would you use in planning professional development activities for your colleagues?

Education Policy

Teachers today work in a climate of exacting demands for accountability. Because some of the policies and processes for holding teachers and schools accountable have been established without much input from teachers, and because unintended consequences of these uninformed courses of action can be damaging (Berliner & Biddle, 1996), it is critical that teachers take steps to influence new developments in educational policy. Teachers can take a leading role in influencing changes in educational policy, not only at the school and district level, but also at the state and national level.

For three years a colleague and I had been team teaching informally, whenever we could make it work. We lobbied our administration for a change in policy that gave priority in scheduling to teachers who were willing to team teach an inclusive class. We argued the change would "put our money where our mouth is"; if we say we want an inclusive school community and high achievement for students with disabilities, we need policies and practices that support that. The new policy has been adopted by both junior high schools in our district.

—Audrey, middle school science teacher

I am a middle level teacher, but I volunteered to be a member of the Pre-Kindergarten Advisory Board, which covers two counties. I have helped to create a dialogue about why universal pre-K is needed and how we can begin to provide it. We are working with our state legislators to allocate funds for a pilot program in our area.

—Tony, seventh-grade social studies teacher

> I became more active in the union at the state level in order to steer it toward being a force for educational change instead of focusing solely on issues related to working conditions and job security.
>
> —Ziporrah, kindergarten teacher

Danielson (2006) notes that teacher leaders are well positioned to bring about change in policies that have a direct impact on students, such as attendance, discipline, homework, and grading policies. To have a voice in the development of policies that will impact you and your students, select one of these actions:

- *Join school site-based teams* such as the shared decision-making team or school leadership team. Teachers in our study reported that through their service on school leadership teams, they helped to bring about changes such as modifying the block schedule and expanding the middle school advisory board to include student representatives.
- *Participate in professional organizations.* Hannah, whose story about leading a challenge to new testing requirements opened this chapter, sought help from the National Association for the Education of Young Children (NAEYC). She was so grateful for the wealth of information she got from their Web site, she decided to join the organization and has been involved with it ever since, serving as membership chair for the regional chapter and as a member of the diversity task force for the state organization. Professional organizations like NAEYC give teachers the information and strategies they need to educate the public, including policy makers, about issues that matter to students and teachers, and consequently to influence policy decisions.
  - Begin by investigating the professional organizations that are relevant to your area of specialization and join one that has an active chapter in your area. You can locate local chapters through the national organizations; contact information for many national organizations is available in Appendix C.
  - Become familiar with the issues through use of the organization's Web site and publications.
  - Consider attending a conference with a colleague and comparing notes about what you can bring back to your school.
  - Look for ways you can contribute your skills to the organization.

- *Learn skills in advocacy.* Advocacy skills can be learned, and teachers have a head start, since we spend our days trying to help people see the truth and act on it. The National Council of Teachers of Mathematics (NCTM) offers members an advocacy toolkit, asserting that "One idea and one voice can make a difference. Collective voices—organized and orchestrated . . . influence decisions. Both politics and education are constantly in a state of change, and you can help shape that change" (NCTM, 2008). Organizations such as the Council for Exceptional Children, the National Council of Teachers of English, the National Science Teachers Association, and National Council for the Social Studies, among others, share NCTM's goals of helping their members learn to advocate effectively so they can contribute to the process of developing sound educational policies.

| Needs Survey, Part 5 | Focus on Policy |

Think about the policies that have a strong influence on your ability to help your students learn. Consider issues such as curriculum mandates, ability tracking, class size, deployment of paraprofessionals, teacher rights and responsibilities, accountability measures, school funding mechanisms and fiscal equity, and any other issue about which you feel strongly.

What structures exist within your school or school district through which teachers can have a voice in developing educational policies (e.g., site-based team, building leadership council, teachers' union)?

- How can you become active within these structures?

What professional organizations represent teachers who share your interests and expertise?

- How can you become a member? (See Appendix C for Web addresses for professional organizations for teachers.)

What can you and your colleagues do to support teacher participation in professional organizations so that your school can benefit from the resources they offer?

Looking Ahead

In Chapter 8, we've reviewed the kinds of changes teachers can make within their multiple spheres of influence. You've had a chance to consider your priorities within each of these spheres and to explore initial steps you might take to address them. How big a leap would it be for you to actually lead others in a change effort? What kinds of skills are needed? In Chapter 9, you'll find out.

CHAPTER 9

Using Classroom-Based Skills to Lead Change

How do I lead a change initiative within my own school? I've gone from being a new teacher to being a senior member of our faculty in just 10 years, and others look to me for ideas and answers. I do have suggestions for how to do things differently. How do I put my ideas out there in a way that invites conversation and promotes action? What skills do I need to inspire others to take risks and do things differently? Where do I begin?

—Jeannine, eighth-grade lead teacher who just completed her National Board certification

Take a few minutes to list people who have inspired you—reach back to your childhood, and continue up through today. Consider the following candidates:

- A public person, whose courage led to changes in the world
- A charismatic relative or friend who knows you very well, someone whose humor, patience, and encouragement enabled you to strive and achieve
- A stirring speaker or writer whose words led you to reflection and action
- A tough coach or mentor who pushed you to achieve new personal bests
- A teacher, friend, or family member who inspired you to take risks

Each of these individuals can help us become leaders. Inspirational individuals whom we only know *about* (through reading their writings or witnessing their accomplishments) enable us to envision new possibilities and can give us the nerve to embark on the journey toward our goals. People we know personally help us by sharing their vision of the person they believe we can become and encouraging us to move forward. What are these role models seeing in us that makes them believe we can lead others to accomplish change initiatives? Essentially, they focus on the same skills we use to be effective teachers.

We make use of our understanding of content and of our students to motivate them to do their best. Motivating our students is a short step away from stimulating our fellow teachers to do things differently.

Teachers base their leadership of change (in schools, professional organizations, and communities) on their own passions to address a specific issue or question and translate their inquiry into action. Here are two examples from the teachers who participated in our survey:

I took my interest in my own garden to the teachers in our sixth grade, who seemed to be struggling to engage their students. I contacted the local cooperative extension so that sixth graders could take advantage of a hydroponic unit in their classroom, to compare and contrast growing plants with or without soil. As a result, we developed a schoolwide garden project. Community members, family members, students, and teachers were involved. It was a great motivator and learning experience for all of us.

—Awilda, third-grade teacher

Parents rarely came to parent-teacher conferences or called about their children's progress, and I wanted them to know what was happening. So I developed an easy-to-use communication form and began using it with my classes. The district had it translated into four languages, and now other teachers use it also.

—Norman, ninth-grade biology teacher

Both these ideas emerged from insights about "What is missing?" and "What resources do I have?" and led to actions that inspired changes in practice. Do you have an insight, idea, or question that could lead to change? Consider how you can translate your idea into action and lead others to change their behavior. To promote the kinds of changes we have described throughout this book, and especially in Chapter 8, you might believe that you need to completely transform yourself, such that you would be surprised at what you see in your professional three-way mirror. You may presume that the skill set required is unfamiliar and beyond your reach.

Nothing could be further from the truth. Learning to inspire others to change is directly related to how you incorporate change into your teaching routine. In this chapter, we will identify how you can build on what you already do to lead change initiatives.

INSPIRING OTHERS TO ACCOMPLISH CHANGE: MIND-SET AND SKILLS

Part of the challenge of leading is getting mentally prepared. Going into a situation prepared to be successful requires envisioning success down to the last detail.

Some situations are easier to envision than others. Imagine yourself getting ready for a new assignment, the class of your dreams. You are a veteran teacher in this building, your students are ready to learn, and you have a high comfort level with the content. What would you do to begin your work with your students, their family members, and others in your building? How different is your outlook from the one you would have if you were taking on a less desirable assignment?

Developing a positive mind-set is an important first step. This chapter will enable you to become confident in your ability to take the next steps, clarifying how you can make use of the skills you use in your teaching to lead others. We believe that with this confidence, your optimistic outlook will become automatic and contagious.

Several of the skills described by David Berliner (1983, 1990) as the "executive functions of teaching" have been used as a springboard to organize this chapter. Each skill set should look very familiar. From your teacher preparation program and onwards, you have taken each of them in stride. Consider how to incorporate these well-used skills in leading change.

MAKING USE OF TEACHING SKILLS TO LEAD CHANGE

Communicate Clearly and Regularly

Communication is like breathing—we take in *and* give out information automatically. Think about the moments throughout the day when you forget other responsibilities while listening to a student or colleague—you are a successful teacher in part because you have learned to listen. You have also learned that giving clear directions to your students, and providing concise feedback, enables you to manage your classroom effectively and help your students to achieve.

Although communication is a skill that most teachers use routinely with their students, school colleagues, and family members of their students, some different nuances are needed to lead and communicate within the context of change. It is important to tailor your communication, motivation, and management strategies to each of the constituencies involved in your change effort. One of the teachers who participated in our research project mentioned that such tailored communication triggers innovation: "Sometimes inspiration is brought on by discussions with (or enthusiasm from) colleagues."

> When doing something new in my classroom, I was reluctant to talk about it. I was afraid people would think I was bragging. As a result, usually my family and friends outside of school were more likely to know about what was going on in my classroom than the teacher next door. When talking with my sister, I got a different perspective. She said that rather than thinking only of myself, I should consider how talking about experiences might benefit others, giving us all sounding boards.
>
> As a result of reflecting on our discussion, I identified a new Wednesday morning routine that included coffee with three teachers—we talk about our classroom innovations. We found that regular brainstorming gives us all a boost. After Thanksgiving, we plan to coordinate an approach among our classrooms, and I volunteered to take the lead. If I hadn't gotten us started, none of this would have taken place.
>
> —Dahlia, high school science teacher who is considering applying for National Board certification

Communication about change initiatives is spontaneous for few people: Most of us must prepare. Without communication, there is little or no spread of ideas and no system-wide adoption of new approaches. Consider this description of the role of communication within change initiatives:

Change is seen first and foremost *as a process of communication*. Initially, a new idea is introduced to a few members of a social system. Through various means of communication, word of the new idea is passed to other members. Over time, most members become aware of the innovation and may adopt it. . . . Knowing who is talking with whom and what is being said about the innovation are important. Identifying the paths along which information is communicated and charting the interpersonal linkages are other important tools. (Hall & Hord, 2006, p. 65, emphasis added)

When you are working on a change initiative in which you want to involve others, begin with the questions that others might ask. Consider sitting down with two or three trusted colleagues at the outset of your initiative. Your conversation need not be complex. Ramsey (1999, p. 172) recommends these five questions for leaders in all situations:

1. What do you want to communicate?

2. Why do you want to communicate this message?

3. Who needs to get the message?

4. How should the message be communicated?

5. When is the best time to communicate it?

These questions can enable you to frame both what and how you want to use communication while leading, as in the examples below.

What: Start by deciding what about your initiative is valuable for others to know. Ragland, Asera, and Johnson (1999) identified characteristics of innovative school districts in Texas. They found that the districts had three themes that characterized their efforts; these three characteristics can help you explain what you want to say: *"urgency, responsibility, and efficacy"* (p. 2).

When you are getting ready to lead a change initiative, give yourself time to think through each of these components before you share your ideas with others. Be prepared to explain what you plan to do. Incorporate into this an explanation of the need (urgency), the role you will take (responsibility), and your confidence that you will see the project through to the end (efficacy).

Why: Teachers who are motivated to lead a change initiative often identify issues related to the students in their classes as the reason for doing things differently. As one of the teachers in our research study explained:

The impetus for change in my professional career has always been linked to a desire to understand where children are coming from, academically, and where they are going next. If teachers are motivated to expand their horizons for the welfare of children, change can be viewed as not only productive, but necessary.

Coming to see all school-based changes, including those that will involve reorganization or expansion of school offerings, as rooted in the needs of the students will enable you to lead change in a way that your faculty colleagues and administrators can understand. Establishing buy-in is an important aspect of involving others in change initiatives.

Who: What makes the difference between those individuals who stay with an effort and those who drop in and out in a way that is inconsistent with the needs of the project? Engaging individuals through the ups and downs is best done by the organization (school, district, or community) as a whole. "Organizational learning" (Collinson, Cook, & Conley, 2006) or "learning organization" (Mohr & Dichter, 2001) both describe the changed climate that instills higher commitment in its members. Wagner (2001) described the outlook that teachers and students have when there is a shared commitment:

> A shared sense of community nurtures active engagement in learning and collaborative problem-solving. Both students and teachers learn more and do more when they feel a part of something important that is larger than themselves and that they have helped to create . . . [at] places in which everyone does much more than the minimum. (p. 383)

To create or tap into the learning community, begin whenever possible by involving your administrators. They will know of district policies and procedures that may have a bearing on your plans; they can connect you with other educators who share your values and ideals; and they may be able to tap resources you cannot access on your own. At best, they will endorse your ideas and champion them, helping you bring them to fruition. If that does not happen, and they are unable to support your idea, do not be discouraged. Take their feedback to rethink your idea. If feasible, pilot your project on a small scale that is within your area of responsibility and look for opportunities to demonstrate its value to your school and community. Make sure to keep your administrators informed. Like you, the majority of administrators want to do what they can to improve student learning; when they see benefits for students, they are likely to come on board.

As you develop your vision for leading change, identify other individuals in your school who are likely to participate in your effort, to create your own broader base. In the planning stage, partner with people interested in your initiative who have different points of view, so that teachers with a variety of experiences can have input into your effort. Brainstorm with them regarding the best way to be heard by a cross section of people within your school.

Once you are confident that you have modified your message successfully, and that it is understood by people who were willing to give you the benefit of the doubt from the outset, it is time to engage others who might be less comfortable working with you on a project like this one, such as the following:

- Skeptics
- Silent people
- Those who "go along to get along"
- Comics
- Mavericks
- Those who are already overcommitted to other responsibilities (at home, at school, in the community)

After you have established some momentum with your change initiative, you will have time to bring these individuals into your effort. Don't try to start with them.

When and How: As we talk with each other about our innovations, we need to think intentionally about when and how we communicate. Hall and Hord (2006) say it this way: "Do not select a classroom that is far off the 'highway' that prospective adopters use frequently. [Select a classroom that] is on the direct route to the staff parking lot or on the way to the staff lounge" (p. 70). Consider Hall and Hord's metaphor as a springboard for sharing information about one of your upcoming change initiatives, using the following Change Challenge.

Change Challenge 9.1 | Mapping the Turf for Sharing the News

Imagine your school building in terms of fertile ground for change. Those are your green spaces; each is an oasis. Consider which areas are the deserts in terms of likelihood for change, and differentiate those from ones in which there is potential. Either actually or in your mind, see how many new green spaces you can create!

Picture your space as it is now: Draw or imagine a map of your school, to visually identify where in your school you will find others to get involved in your change initiative.

Picture your space as it might be: Either actually or in your mind, color the rooms according to your evaluation of each room as *being open to* your change effort.

Then, creatively "draw your highways" between the oases, indicating not only the point-to-point connections, but also how you can communicate about what you are doing. Read through the options below, and then pick your favorite two choices.

- *Billboards:* Post information outside your room that highlights success stories about your change initiatives.
- *Speed Traps*: Get people to slow down enough to respond to a "Question of the week" that pertains to what you and your students are doing in your classroom. Work with your students to attractively summarize the answers from the students, teachers, and others in your building who have answered your question.
- *Rent-a-Vehicle*: Give passersby opportunities to try out the change initiative you have begun.
- *Construction Zone*: Post information elsewhere in your school, or on your classroom or school Web site, explaining what you are trying to do, when your change initiative will conclude, and the progress you are making. This "under construction" information can help others to see that the work you are doing is "in progress" and not something that happens all at once.

Note how you will implement your "highway project" in the space provided below.

Selection 1:

Selection 2:

As you become more comfortable with seeing your initiatives as part of a broader effort—to create more "green spaces" in your building, or in your community—you will find yourself becoming less focused on yourself and more on the impact your effort is having. As a result, you are likely to become more confident when sharing information about your classroom. Use this kind of thinking to differentiate your communication for each of the constituencies to be involved in the effort.

Motivate People to Take Risks and Accept Challenges

Cherry and Spiegel (2006) encourage us to "reframe our understandings about leadership by way of Oz" (p. 71), using familiar characters from L. Frank Baum's book as examples of personal transformation. The authors encourage us to use this metaphor to explore different leadership models. For example, they view the Tin Man as analogous to Robert Evans's model of leadership that emphasizes authenticity and integrity; they link the Cowardly Lion's search to Bolman and Deal's "courageous exploration into the spiritual underpinnings of leadership" (p. 76). Dorothy's journey along the yellow brick road is an alternate path to leadership as described by Cherry and Spiegel, one "that leads to the creation of visual or tangible images derived by way of storytelling and metaphor" (p. 76).

Cherry and Spiegel encourage school leaders to make use of metaphor for analysis and ultimately to engage others. The process of motivating others, and encouraging them to take risks, involves helping them understand the effort in which we hope to engage them. The process of reflection used throughout this book, combined with planning and implementing a change initiative (see Chapter 6–7 for details), can lead to inviting others into the initiative. Select one of the following options (or combine them) to engage your fellow teachers:

- *Metaphor Process:* Create a metaphor that explains the change initiative, using a popular book, song, or film. Use it to think through and highlight vital parts of your initiative.
- *Analytical Invitation:* List the pros and cons you have identified—what are you and your students getting out of the effort, as compared to what would happen if you'd left things alone?
- *Cost/Benefit Analysis:* Show the amount of time and energy you've invested in your initiative, as well as the outcomes achieved.
- *Moral Persuasion:* Enable the individuals with whom you work to examine the needs of students for whom the change initiative will be highly beneficial.

Hargreaves's hard-hitting analysis of "contrived collegiality" (1994) underscores the need to encourage authentic collaboration, which he characterizes as "spontaneous, voluntary, development-oriented, pervasive across time and space, and unpredictable" (pp. 192–193) and the opposite of "administratively regulated" or "compulsory" (p. 195). Engaging individuals in meaningful change initiatives requires that they clearly locate the proposed initiative within the context of their own value system and believe it has the potential to achieve its goals. Sergiovanni (2000) describes this engagement process as evidence that "collegial values and shared decision making are present" (p. 133). Make use of the most appealing of the options above to engage others in your effort. Help them invest in new initiatives that advance service delivery for students or will help teachers achieve their professional goals.

Be Proactive in Problem Solving

In many ways, effective teachers are first and foremost outstanding problem solvers. Consider Stipek's (2006) description of the characteristics of effective preschool teachers:

Good teachers are busy asking questions, focusing children's attention, helping them document and interpret what they see, and providing scaffolds and suggestions . . .

Effective teachers also maintain children's enthusiasm for learning by being vigilant and seizing opportunities to use children's interests. (p. 742)

When we revise the paragraph, replacing *teachers* and *children* with *leaders* and *colleagues,* it is easy to see parallels between the problem-solving skills of teachers and change leaders:

Good *leaders* are busy asking questions, focusing *colleagues'* attention, helping them document and interpret what they see, and providing scaffolds and suggestions . . .

Effective *leaders* also maintain *colleagues'* enthusiasm . . . by being vigilant and seizing opportunities to use *colleagues'* interests.

Classroom skills are easily translated into those needed to make change happen. Through individualization, effective interaction strategies, and engaging others by building on their interests and enthusiasm, you can bring others into your problem-solving process. You can make use of the problem-solving strategies you use in your classroom to walk others through the steps of anticipating and resolving problems with your change initiative.

Of course, there are some differences between what you do in the classroom and what is happening when engaging others in a change effort. Both Ramsey (1999) and Cochran-Smith (2005) discuss the need to address politics when undertaking an initiative, and politics are not always part of classroom instruction. Although we may wish that politics could be handled by someone else, we must be alert to the potential for losing momentum, time, and energy if we do not correctly position a change initiative. Developing a sound footing for a change initiative, via buy-in from the necessary formal leaders (e.g., administrators, officers of the union, or parent organizations) as well as those who are the informal leaders (e.g., individuals who have no specific titles, but are visible and vocal), is essential. One way to accomplish this is to try a pilot version of your initiative. As one of the participants in our research survey cautioned, "Go slow. Think it through. Talk to others who have made the change. Make provisions to try it out before buying it completely. Get your facts and be totally prepared."

Establishing a routine for identifying problems, and preventing them, links to the politics of the situation. Some problems emerge because there has been insufficient attention paid to getting resources in advance, while others are a result of dealing with unexpected aspects of the situation (Hall & Hord, 2006).

> I learn when I am ready to really get started on a project through my ride to work. Before I am ready, I go through all of these "what if?" questions—and I keep coming up with new questions. I know I am ready when all the questions I come up with I've thought of before, and I begin to plan when I'll go ahead. I take a deep breath when this happens and think to myself, "Now I can get started."
>
> —Mark, 15-year high school math teacher

MAKING USE OF TEACHING SKILLS TO SUSTAIN CHANGE

Hall and Hord (2006) identify two key steps for leading change initiatives after you have gotten them underway: progress monitoring and providing continual assistance. For teachers, these are not new concepts. You have a history of success: Consider your history as a database of ideas to adapt as you learn to lead others in change.

Check on Progress

Monitoring and assessing progress is one of the responsibilities that teachers have in common with business executives (Berliner, 1983). Teachers learn to measure incremental change, so they can stay on top of where progress is being made and where it needs to be nudged along or guided back onto the right track. In leading a change project, we must find ways to monitor and assess the work that is taking place within the initiative; this way, we can determine whether successful movement is taking place or if the project is stuck. To check on progress of colleagues, ask specific questions periodically while the change effort is underway. Conversations that focus on monitoring the change initiative can have the same effect as determining whether your students are on the right track. Rather than waiting until the end, with a summative evaluation, approach leadership formatively, gathering data throughout the effort.

One caveat about progress monitoring while leading change: Avoid the guilt trap. Develop an approach (e.g., stopping by the classroom of participating teachers, arranging for short meetings) that will not involve additional lag time (e.g., e-mailing, leaving a phone message) and possibly require additional follow-up. Streamline the process for checking in with others, so that you remain informed. Hargreaves (1994) explains that "guilt is a central emotional preoccupation for teachers. It recurs frequently when they are asked to talk about their work and their relation to it. . . . 'Teaching is a profession that you go home, you always have stuff that you think about. You think, "I should be doing this"[or] 'I feel guilty sitting down half the time'" (p. 142). Guilt can be counterproductive and prevent progress.

Leading others in a change initiative will likely be wedged in among other aspects of your role as a teacher; therefore, progress monitoring must be circumscribed. The goal for teacher leaders in measuring progress is to encourage regular monitoring that becomes part of the routine of all involved in the project, not just the leader. Teachers find the effort worthwhile because change efforts have the potential to be extremely satisfying. Over 80% of the teachers who participated in our research study indicated that changes they experienced were made voluntarily at least half of the time, and only a few judged the impact of change to be negative for teachers (5%) or students (8%).

Change Challenge 9.2 Maintaining Perspective

Think back to a time when you saw a fellow teacher trying to do too much. List four or five guidelines you would advise your fellow teacher to consider to keep things in perspective. Use these words of advice when you become overly ambitious as a teacher leader.

1. _____

2. _____

3. _____

4. _____

5. _____

Provide Continuous Assistance

Teacher leaders provide authentic encouragement for colleagues, so all know they are not in this effort alone. But they don't stop there; they provide whatever help is needed, from additional resources to hands-on assistance. Huberman & Miles (1984) describe the important role that colleague teachers can have during school reform, based on their field sample at 12 different schools. They discussed the emerging roles of teacher leaders, who provided different types of assistance, differentiated over the cycle of the innovation (p. 104). "[Huberman and Miles] noted that a group of teacher leaders—whom they called *enforcers*—often provide resources and encouragement to other teachers for adopting a new practice. Enforcers understand the innovation and are invested in its continued use" (Sindelar, Shearer, Yendol-Hoppey, & Liebert, 2006, p. 318). Consider using one of these strategies to support others:

- Regularly "check the pulse" of the people with whom you are working, to see what kind of help they need or want to solve their problems. This assures people that you value their efforts, that their efforts are important, and that they have supports available to them.
- Try a "one-legged" interview—a hallway conversation between you and the person you are helping to change that lasts only about as long as you can stand on one leg.
- Enable your fellow teachers to develop "going right" and "going wrong" signals to inform you of a need for touching base. This can be as simple as leaving a particular playing card in your mail box to let you know to stop by—the red card might let you know there is a problem, and the black that something you might like to hear about has gone well. A different number for each classroom will enable you to know who requested a visit.

Differentiate between "one-way" and "two-way" contacts, to be able to clarify expectations and to stay in continuous communication without overburdening recipients.

"One ways" are clearly designated as emotional supports or pats on the back or as "FYI"—no response is needed or expected. Providing regular encouragement is part of assistance, so that teachers know that their work is not invisible.

"Two ways" are questions or requests for assistance that need a response within 24 hours. Providing prompt responses is one of the most important aspects of a leader. Enable teachers to understand that you got their message and that you will respond quickly.

Failure to check progress and follow up is cause for failure of many change efforts. Discuss the plan for follow-up with teachers in advance, so that your approach is coordinated and understood by all.

When in Florida, I taught in a year-round school where we were in session for 11 months. Three times during the year, students had two weeks in a row where they could either come to a program called "intersession" or take the two weeks off as a breather. Likewise, teachers could opt to teach for extra pay, or take the time off. I taught all three of these intersessions. It was a totally different kind of teaching. Each team of teachers consisted of six teachers of three different grade levels, and we would integrate all of the kids and teach in themes, like *Under the Sea* or *Africa*.

We had to develop strategies for communication and support, because everything was so condensed. We rotated the role of *problem solver*, to make sure that everyone had a chance to give a daily update and ask for help if needed. We had so little time, it was like running a relay for the two weeks. But we found that doing many things to share news about our students' successes (e.g., texting, different colored notes outside our doors, and quick conversations at the end of the day) enabled us to support each other throughout the two weeks. During the regular school year, we stayed in touch and incorporated shared resources on a joint unit on birds. We used a weekly rotating leadership model to stay positive and provide help to each other.

—Tina, fourth-grade teacher

Consider the following Change Challenge to assess progress for two completed initiatives—one in which you take pride, and another which you know could have been better. You may find surprises as you evaluate each one, using the criteria of Collinson, Cook, and Conley (2006). This could focus your next effort.

Change Challenge 9.3	Reflecting and Reassessing

Think of your school, district, or community at two points in time: one when you felt that things went as well as possible (Best), and one when things did not go so well (Improvement needed). Grade your organization, using an A–F rating scale for each condition identified by Collinson et al. and select one on which to focus when leading your next initiative.

Example by Diana:

Our school held a very successful Odyssey of the Mind, but a much less successful after-school tutoring program. I used the Odyssey to assign all the "Best" grades below, and the tutoring program for all the "Improvement needed" grades below. After completing this exercise, I found that there were some criteria on which the less successful program got a better grade—helping me to look more carefully at each program, rather than assuming one was great and the other one not so good.

1. Prioritizing learning for all members
    a. Best ____
    b. Improvement needed ____

2. Facilitating the dissemination (sharing of knowledge, skills, and insights)
    a. Best ____
    b. Improvement needed ____

3. Attending to human relationships
    a. Best ____
    b. Improvement needed ____

(Continued)

(Continued)

    4. Fostering inquiry
       a. Best ___
       b. Improvement needed ___

    5. Enhancing democratic governance
       a. Best ___
       b. Improvement needed ___

    6. Providing for members' self-fulfillment
       a. Best ___
       b. Improvement needed ___

Now, look over your responses to Change Challenge 9.3. Circle the item that you'd like to make sure gets incorporated into the next initiative you undertake in your school, district, or community.

If you are able to make a difference in the item you circled above, you might be able to bring around a reluctant teacher or keep a teacher involved during the initiative's ups and downs. Craig (2006) describes the transition a single teacher made, from being unwilling to participate in a change initiative in a school (his response consistently was "no comment" when asked for his input) to his new outlook, when he volunteered to participate. The teacher eventually became part of one of the "knowledge communities" Craig studied; she investigated many examples of teacher-based stories about school reform (Craig, 2001). You might see a similar change in an individual or group before, during, and after your change initiative.

Remember What Matters Most

In this chapter we have shown how you can lead change by using the teaching skills you already possess. Just as important as teaching skills are the core beliefs about teaching and learning that you bring to the change effort (Pickering, 2006). We can change, and can help others to do so, to the extent that the expected results are important to us. We can rise to the challenge of leading change when the new undertaking is tied to our highest aspirations for our students.

Looking Ahead

Chapter 9 was intended to demystify the process of leading a change initiative. Highlighting the use you make of your reflection, and the adaptation you can make of your current skills, the chapter was designed to both give you a realistic vision of yourself as a leader of change and inspire you to take on the challenge. Chapter 10 will enable you to see your work with change within the context of your entire career.

PART V

Changing Throughout a Teaching Career

The final part of *A Teacher's Guide to Change* encourages teachers to see change as an opportunity for professional development and stimulation that is essential for sustained vitality in a teaching career. In Chapter 10, we explore the changes that signal transition from one phase of a career to the next and urge teachers to reach out to their colleagues, to both offer and receive help in navigating these changes. Expanding our roles, for example as mentors to a new generation of teachers, enables us to continue to find gratification in our work; more importantly, it ensures that students will continue to benefit from teachers who regularly renew themselves and their commitment to the profession.

CHAPTER 10

Sustaining Career
Vitality Through Change

- "I gave up my tenure after 18 years to pursue my goal of being a special education teacher in the district."
- "I have requested, and received, an honors class."
- "I have established cooperative relationships with ophthalmologists who provide services to my students with visual impairments."
- "I found ways to alternatively assess my students with disabilities other than paper and pencil, mostly through the use of cameras and camcorders, to definitively show people outside the class that the students have mastered their goals and objectives, and met the state standards."

While teachers' careers unfold, many seek innovative options, undertaking new initiatives to better meet students' needs or to advance school reform. The challenges, reasons, and resources for change differ throughout our careers. This chapter highlights the developmental life cycle for teachers and underscores some of the opportunities teachers are drawn toward across their careers.

In their classic study, *The Lives of Teachers* (1993), Huberman, Grounauer, and Marti identify numerous versions of the life cycles of teachers, always following a sequence that includes the following:

- Phase 1: "Feeling one's way" at the beginning, which can either be easy *or* painful
- Phase 2: Stabilization and consolidation *or* self doubt
- Phase 3: Pursuit (acquired wisdom, sense of well-being) *or* detachment (loss of enthusiasm, withdrawal)
- Retirement, with either serenity *or* bitterness

Huberman's exploration of the examinations of teachers' evolution (in coauthored studies in 1984 and 1993) has served as a basis for further study by many other researchers (e.g., Little, 1990, 2001; Hargreaves 2000, 2005), who examined what happens between our first interest in teaching and our last day in the classroom. What is it about change that draws us at different stages of our careers?

As teachers, we live with the dichotomies of change throughout our careers, with change stimulating us to consider different options. As Bascia and Hargreaves (2000) point out, the challenging side of change can drive teachers out of the profession:

> Educators find themselves working in a deeply paradoxical profession where, on the one hand, they are hailed as the catalysts of change, the harbingers of the new informational society, the creators of the knowledge and learning on which success in this society will depend. . . . On the other hand, teachers are also the casualties of the informational society with its commitment to individual skilling, personal lifestyle, consumer preference, market driven influences. (p. 20)

This duality was also noted by Little (2001): "Reform both stimulates teacher enthusiasm and results in burnout, expands some learning opportunities and erodes others, intensifies professional bonds and foments professional conflict" (p. 28).

To prevent teachers from becoming casualties, Bascia & Hargreaves (2000) urge us to act: "It is about time that teachers were pulled back from the sharp edge of change and moved toward its leading edge—intellectually, emotionally, and politically" (p. 20). What would this consist of at different points in our careers?

THE EARLY YEARS: GAINING A SENSE OF OURSELVES AS TEACHERS

As we begin our lives as teachers, we are vulnerable. As Mandel (2006) explains, "New teachers are not thinking about raising scores on the standardized test in May; they are more concerned about getting through fifth period tomorrow. First year teachers have one basic goal in mind—survival . . . And much of what new teachers need can only be provided through supportive interaction with veteran teachers" (pp. 66–67). Early in their careers, new teachers are beginning to "create a professional identity and mission that helps them make a difference in the lives of those they teach that . . . helps teachers overcome the demands of this rewarding, yet draining, profession" (Smith, Petty, & Day, 2008, p. 29).

Consider the following example:

> My mother and her two sisters were teachers, and I honestly never considered another career choice. From the time I was a little girl, I would always play "school," making sure that I was the teacher. So imagine my shock and shame when I found myself crying myself to sleep for the first two months of my life as a first-year teacher because I knew I had no control over my classroom. I kept thinking, "Is this really what I thought I wanted to do?" In November, I walked into my class one day smiling and my seventh graders were shocked—they had never seen me smile before. Their amazed comments led me right down the hall to one of the master teachers. I asked for her help, and it saved me from quitting.
>
> —Alexia, 12th year veteran, lead teacher in charge of new teacher orientation

This teacher knew she had to adjust her outlook, and rethink her instructional and management strategies. She could not go on without help. And haven't we all been at that point in our lives, when "getting through" was the most we could expect from ourselves? Huberman et al. (1993) illustrate that whether individuals have easy or difficult beginnings, they must reach a point of "stabilization" before they begin to experiment or get involved in change.

The development of the Interstate New Teacher Assessment and Support Consortium (INTASC) standards in 1992, adopted as the guide for teacher evaluation by many professional organizations, specified useful principles that new teachers can strive to achieve during their induction period. Johnson (2001) explains the spread of the INTASC standards:

> In a move to strengthen the teaching profession, the influential National Commission on Teaching and America's Future recommended that all schools of education be accredited by the National Council for Accreditation of Teacher Education (NCATE) and that all state licensing of individual teachers conform to standards set by the Interstate New Teacher Assessment and Support Consortium (INTASC). (p. 395)

This movement has clarified the responsibilities of teacher education departments, and the INTASC standards became embedded in the standards of many professional organizations, with the goal of enabling new teachers to start their careers better prepared to meet their responsibilities. However, more is needed, in part because those entering today's teaching career path differ from their mentors, as Johnson et al. (2004) observe: The generation of teachers today "is not simply a younger version of the retiring generation; it is a different generation altogether . . . less accepting of top-down hierarchy and fixed channels of communication, less respectful of conventional organizations, and generally more entrepreneurial than their predecessors" (p. 252).

Professional organizations are reaching out to this new generation of beginning teachers in ways tailored to address them, often using technology. They offer resources aimed at the start-up concerns, such as blogs for new teachers on professional Web sites, and Webinars throughout the first year. These strategies can enable new teachers to connect to professional organizations more readily, and from there to access professional development opportunities.

As new participants in professional development, beginning teachers benefit from an observation made by Easton (2008) of the shift from "training" to "development" for teachers:

> Development activities . . . are neither bad nor wrong. In some cases they are vital to professional and organizational growth. But they are not sufficient. If all educators needed to do was develop (i.e., grow, expand, advance, progress, mature, enlarge, or improve), perhaps development would be enough. But educators often find that more and better are not enough. They find they often need to change what they do, on a daily or sometimes hourly basis, as they respond to the needs of the learners they serve. (p. 755)

The search for "the solution" is often a panic-driven response to a classroom problem, rather than an examination of multiple options. Beginning teachers can benefit from the advice of Hargreaves (2005): "the three m's of sustainable educational change—*mixture* (of teacher age groups), *mentoring* (across the generations) and *memory* (conscious collective learning from wisdom and experience)" (p. 982). Participation in the mentoring process within schools can enable beginning teachers to participate in a network with others who can recall their own experiences with the start of the teaching career. But mentoring needs to take advantage of new approaches. Consider the value of the "Move Me On" column published in *Teaching History*, a publication of The Historical Association (Great Britain): Situations encountered by new history teachers are addressed by multiple mentors, facilitating consideration of several viewpoints.

The challenge for teachers reading this book is to engage their newer colleagues in ways that are relevant to them. Consider this Change Challenge as a way to begin.

Change Challenge 10.1   Getting to Know Young Colleagues

Over the course of the year, take time to have a conversation with some new teachers. Get their input about the strategies they use for the following:

- Staying connected with their friends
- Finding information about leisure activities (e.g., movie reviews, sports, ticket purchases, equipment sales, etc.)
- Professional development
- Developing their own Web sites or blogs
- Getting information for their personal lives (e.g., recipes, health, local services, etc.)
- Getting information for use in their classes

As you consider working with newer teachers on change initiatives, explore using one of the strategies that will appeal to younger teachers.

THE MIDDLE YEARS: MAKING THE TRANSITION FROM MENTEE TO MENTOR

As we become more experienced teachers, we may become engaged in what Little and Bartlett (2002) called the "innovation bubbles [based in] professional community" in which we "persist in collaborative, innovative activity against the odds and largely against the grain of the institution—sometimes for long periods of time" (p. 351). The engagement of teachers within their schools and professional organizations can be seen in the "teacher learning community" described by McLaughlin and Talbert (2001), which demonstrated "values consistent with mutual support and innovation, together with a flexible stance toward subject and a commitment to student learning" (Little and Bartlett, 2002, p. 352).

It is during the middle of our careers that we engage in new roles, as teacher leaders or as mentors. Consider the following account, in which a volunteer mentor recognizes that his primary role is change agent.

Getting her to stop blaming the kids for not learning—that's the key. I have to bring her around to seeing her role in the problems she's having. She says they're unmotivated, disinterested, can't be bothered to do their homework. I see my job here as helping her recognize that these same kids are doing just fine in other classes; that the difference is in her approach to them, and that has to change before anything else can.

It's tricky. I have to be diplomatic. I focus on the positives and point out the successes she's had. I tell little stories from my classes to help her to see the good in these kids. I'm trying to get her to take a broader view of our roles as teachers, to see that it is so much more than covering the content.

I don't want to alienate her. I want to offer her support, give her suggestions, but in a collegial way. Right now it's not working. Without saying so directly, she's implying that if other teachers are not having problems with these students, it's because their standards are low. I'm trying not to take offense. I plan to be persistent and stay optimistic. We are a rural school district, and it is hard to get any new teachers to come here, let alone bright ones who are fully certified. So I'm going to keep at it, and try to help her turn it around.

—Joe, a middle school science teacher and unofficial
mentor to a struggling second-year teacher

The fact that Joe assumed his mentoring responsibilities without recognition or compensation is not unusual. In examining teacher leaders, Martin (2007) encouraged us to think beyond titles:

There are layers of leadership distributed throughout the school, each in an area of expertise and comfort zone . . . two layers of [formal] teacher leadership: those who are assigned and those who volunteer. A third layer is more informal, consisting of teachers who lead in the framework of their classrooms. (p. 17)

She highlights the numerous opportunities that exist for mid-career teachers to take on roles as teacher leaders, based on their increased content knowledge or leadership style (e.g., department heads, literacy coaches, mentors, staff development, data interpretation) without necessarily moving to exclusively administrative roles.

Each of these more advanced roles (especially the direct or indirect mentor) has its own unique benefits, unavailable to the beginning teacher. Hanson and Moir (2008) interviewed 50 former mentors about their experiences serving as mentors and found that 91% remained in their districts five to nine years after serving as mentors. In reflection, mentors' comments led the researchers to identify several common themes, including "mentoring broadens teachers' views of themselves and the teaching profession" and "mentoring deepens teachers' understanding of teaching and learning" (p. 455). The benefits of mentoring generally focus on the mentee, but the mentor can also be a beneficiary. Mentoring does not remain the same across the career of either the mentor or the mentee, although there are some constants. Bouquillon, Sosik, and Lee (2005) found that the mentees in educational settings were significantly more likely to evolve their working relationship into more of a peer relationship than mentees in business settings:

Trust develops over time as the mentoring relationship matures into a peer-like friendship and becomes less of a hierarchical counseling relationship. Educational settings provide a collegial and nurturing environment that facilitates the emergence of strong bonds of trust that support the provision of psychosocial support functions including acceptance, confirmation and friendship. (p. 252)

Teachers who are ready to serve as mentors might consider doing so in a new context, such as in an online community like the one studied by Vavasseur and MacGregor (2008). They found increased levels of communication, collaboration, and reflection when online communities were created to supplement the face-to-face interactions that take place in schools.

Complete the Change Challenge below to explore becoming a mentor.

Change Challenge 10.2   Seeing Yourself as a Mentor

Check off all descriptors below that you feel you *currently* could offer as a mentor. Then, underline any abilities and qualities that you *would like to develop*.

- ❏ *Understanding*—communicating empathy to mentee
- ❏ *Supportive*—providing encouragement
- ❏ *Curricular suggestions*—ability to provide constructive suggestions for mentee in reorganizing lessons and provide a sound rationale
- ❏ *Sense of humor*—when times are tough, knowing when and how to lighten things up
- ❏ *Provide resources*—good at referring mentee to resources available through the Web or in local libraries or resource centers
- ❏ *Help stimulate a reflective process*—asking thought-provoking questions

---

THE LATER YEARS: EXPANDING OUR ROLES

As we develop our classroom talents, we are able to become involved in more and more change initiatives—sometimes to our own surprise, as Sabata's story shows:

When I began teaching, I joined a teacher Web group that had threaded discussions for new teachers. When I was most frustrated, my unseen fellow teachers (some new, some more experienced) had encouraging words and practical suggestions. Over the years I stayed involved, gradually shifting from mostly asking for help to mostly offering it and providing a sympathetic ear. Then a casual conversation with my principal led to discussion about this support system, and to the benefits of an anonymous system in general. I had a tech-savvy student teacher at the time, and we were able to work together to set up a districtwide discussion board that teachers could participate in anonymously. It has gained in popularity and usefulness over time. I was amazed to realize that I had gone from recipient to contributor to designer of a Web-based resource.

—Sabata, elementary special education teacher

Each time we embark on a new project that requires us to change, we should recognize that we are increasingly ready to tackle what is difficult to do. With each new undertaking, we should become more confident about our ability to assume expanded roles within our schools, our communities, and our profession. Consider the challenge below as an exploration of how teachers mature into new roles.

Change Challenge 10.3	Cataloging Change

Review the changes listed below and place a check mark next to all that you have been involved with in the past five years. Draw a circle around any that you would like to be involved with in the next five years (even if it already has a check mark beside it).

- ❏ Changing grade levels
- ❏ Changing (or expanding to an additional) content areas
- ❏ Making a major change in instructional practice
- ❏ Supervising a student teacher
- ❏ Serving as a mentor to a new teacher
- ❏ Developing a new way to involve my students' families within my classroom
- ❏ Working on a schoolwide project
- ❏ Moving to a new district
- ❏ Working with a coteacher in my classroom
- ❏ Coordinating with a teacher in a different classroom on a joint project
- ❏ Helping my students to work with students in another classroom in our building
- ❏ Helping my students to work with students in other locations
- ❏ Helping students to do volunteer work in our community
- ❏ Involving family members in schoolwide activities
- ❏ Working with community members to develop opportunities and resources for students
- ❏ Working with community members and my students to provide services to our community
- ❏ Working with community members and my students to provide services to another community

In an article by Seaton, Emmett, Welsh and Petrossian (2008), each of the authors presents a different point of view on creating instructional leadership teams. Emmett, the teacher author, makes the following comment: "The greatest hurdle is introducing change in the school. It has been a tricky balancing act between pushing and supporting staff members to do things differently, whether in a faculty meeting or in their classroom" (p. 29).

How do we become better at encouraging others to take risks? Lopez-Real and Kwan (2005) found, after surveying 259 university teacher mentors in Hong Kong, that the biggest resource for learning while mentoring was self-reflection:

Because many of the mentors perceive themselves to be in the position of role model and advisor, they feel compelled to examine their own teaching approaches, techniques, attitudes, etc., in greater depth and more critically than they might normally do. . . . The second avenue for self-reflection appears to arise from the observation of the student teachers' lessons and the need to provide feed-back. This can lead the mentor to analyze the differences between the student teachers' performance and their own. (pp. 22–23)

Self-reflection is a strategy that becomes increasingly automatic as we advance in our careers.

As Huberman and Miles (1984) describe, the senior teacher is addressing different challenges from those of beginning or mid-career teachers. Some may be disillusioned with worsening conditions, which can include unmotivated students, administrative burdens, fatigue, or disagreement with official policies. At the same time, other teachers may experience the fruits of reform, including interest in taking on more responsibilities, attempting pedagogical experimentation, and interest in collaboration with colleagues. There is no single way to predict who will become teachers with a positive, optimistic outlook and who will develop a bias toward the negative. External factors influencing these outlooks include type of school, difficulty of assignment, available resources, and availability of support outside of school; internal factors include confidence, fear of the unknown, prior experience, and comfort with change. All of these can contribute to the kind of resolution teachers experience as they near the end of their careers.

An interesting look at options is offered by Intrator and Kunzman (2006), who suggest that teachers must always explore the aspirational goals we have for our work with our students. In their article about professional development, they encourage us to pursue these goals:

Teachers yearn for professional development experiences that not only advance their skills and knowledge base but also simultaneously probe their sense of purpose and invite deliberation about what matters most in good teaching. Evoking the inner life of our teachers—that is, engaging teachers in activities that cultivate their capacity to teach with greater consciousness, self-awareness, and integrity—is a necessary condition . . . for rekindling the sense of passion and purpose essential for . . . growth over the long haul. (p. 39)

Rekindling our passion is the challenge for us at many points throughout our careers, and the tinder of change and reform enables us to look at the best way to engage ourselves in inquiry that leads to improved practice. Hargreaves (2000) warns us:

Many teachers caught up in educational reform and change are experiencing increasing role expansion and role diffuseness, with no sense of where their commitments and responsibilities should end. . . . Teacher professionalism and professional learning are at the crossroads—becoming more extended and collegial in some ways, more exploitative and overextended in others. The puzzle and the challenge for educators and policy-makers is how to build strong professional communities in teaching that are authentic, well supported, and include fundamental purposes, and benefit teachers and students alike. (p. 166)

LOOKING TO THE FUTURE

A Teacher's Guide to Change has been designed to spark your thoughtful reflection on how you can develop a pragmatic commitment to change. As the examples throughout this book have shown, change is likely to infuse our lives as teachers. Once we learn to approach it with confidence and optimism, it can become for us as essential as oxygen. We urge you to take advantage of the air of change at all times in your career: Find ways to motivate yourself and others to breathe deeply.

Appendixes

Appendix A

Survey Items and Responses

Introduction to the survey

As a teacher, you have likely experienced many changes over the years. Some may have resulted from choices you made (e.g., relocating to a new city, taking on extracurricular responsibilities) and some may have been outside your control (e.g., new state standards influenced your curriculum, new administrators were hired for your school). This anonymous survey has been designed to gather information about the kinds of change teachers experience, the strategies they use to respond to change, and the impact change has on teachers. The survey, which most people finish in about 20 minutes, must be completed in a single sitting and should be done within two weeks from the time you receive it. We hope you will agree to complete the survey, to allow others to benefit from your experiences with change. Your responses will be completely anonymous. Please click "Start Survey" to begin.

Request for informed consent

This survey has been developed by Sharon Cramer, Ph.D., Buffalo State College, and Jan Stivers, Ph.D., Marist College, who are studying how teachers manage the inevitable change they encounter in their professional lives. We are collecting responses from teachers across the United States, and plan to use the results and the comments we obtain through this survey in a book on teachers and change to be published by Corwin in 2009.

You are being asked to participate in this survey because a teacher educator has nominated you as an experienced teacher who will provide thoughtful responses to the survey questions.

There are no anticipated risks associated with completion of this survey. The survey has 22 questions; most ask you to select your responses from a list of options, and some ask for short answers.

Please note that if you have "disabled cookies" on your computer to block pop-ups, you will need to "enable cookies" in order to participate in this survey.

Our research design and this survey have been approved by the Institutional Review Board at Buffalo State College and Marist College, to ensure compliance with proper research standards. **Your responses are confidential and no information that can be used to identify you will be gathered.** Once you submit your answers, they are stored within the Zoomerang.com site and cannot be linked to you personally. If you volunteer information during any part of the research project, it will be held in strict confidence by the researchers. If we select a comment you offer in the survey as an example for our book, we will disguise it so it cannot be linked to you or your school.

You do not have to respond to the survey and there are no penalties or negative consequences if you do not participate. If you agree to participate, you can skip any questions you'd prefer not to answer, with the exception of the first two questions (which establish your consent and your eligibility to participate). At the end of the survey you will be given an opportunity to participate in a follow-up phone interview. The interview would take approximately 15 minutes and the same guarantees of confidentiality are assured.

If you have any questions or comments about this research, or if you would like to receive a copy of the results, please contact Sharon Cramer (cramersf@buffalostate.edu) or Jan Stivers (Jan.Stivers@Marist.edu)

Thank you for your time and effort. If you have read and understand the information above, and if you consent to participate in this research, please begin the survey by answering question 1 below.

(Note: The number in the first column of each answer is the count of respondents selecting the option; the number in the second column is the percentage of the total respondents selecting the option.)

1. I have read and I understand the information above, and so indicate by answering "yes" below.

   Yes   121   100%

   No   0   0%

2. How many years total have you been teaching? (If you took a break from teaching for several years, subtract those years to derive your total number of years.)

   *3 years and under   8   7%

   4 to 10 years   29   25%

   11 to 20 years   41   35%

   21 years and over   40   34%

   Note: These teachers did not meet the criteria for inclusion in the study and were offered no further items on this survey.

3. Please select all the experiences below that have been part of your career as a teacher.

   Change in grade level or content specialization   93   84%

   Change in student populations (e.g., disability, ethnicity,   82   74%
   socioeconomic status, other)

	70	63%
Change in own role within the school (e.g., coteacher, team leader)	70	63%
Change in relationships with teaching colleagues (e.g., additions, departures, interpersonal conflict)	91	82%
Mandated curriculum change	79	71%
Change in administration	97	87%
Move to new district	58	52%
Pursuing graduate degree(s)	68	62%
Other: please briefly describe	28	25%

4. When you reflect on the changes that have been part of your experience as a teacher, how would you characterize the major changes overall?

Note: Top number is the count of respondents selecting the option. Bottom number is the percentage of the total respondents selecting the option.

	All or most of the time	About half of the time	Seldom or never
Voluntary	29 26%	62 56%	19 17%
Anticipated	36 34%	59 56%	10 10%
Welcome	28 27%	69 66%	7 7%
Simple to manage	19 18%	64 62%	20 19%
Having significant impact	52 50%	47 45%	5 5%

5. How would you characterize the overall impact of these changes, on your students and on yourself?

Note: Top number is the count of respondents selecting the option. Bottom number is the percentage of the total respondents selecting the option.

	Mostly beneficial	Mostly neutral	Mostly harmful
Students	58 53%	43 39%	9 8%
Yourself	65 61%	37 35%	5 5%

6. Indicate all the types of changes you have experienced in your home and family situations over the course of your teaching career.

Marriage	62	57%
Divorce	17	16%
Remarriage	11	10%
Addition of one or more children	65	60%
Change in childrearing or other family responsibilities	45	42%
Relocation	63	58%
Major change in economic circumstances	41	38%
Major illness (affecting you or a member of your household)	28	26%
Major illness of a member of your extended family	49	45%
Death of a family member	66	61%
Other: please briefly explain	20	19%

7. On average, how often did a change (such as the personal and professional ones listed above) impact you? Select the best answer from the choices below.

Every few months	6	5%
Once or twice per year	27	25%
Every two or three years	43	39%
Less than every three years	34	31%

8. During your teaching career, have you experienced a professional or personal change that had a major **positive impact** on you as a teacher?

Yes	93	88%
No	13	12%
Total	106	100%

Additional narrative responses: 93

9. During your teaching career, have you experienced a professional or personal change that had a major **negative impact** on you as a teacher?

Yes	74	70%
No	32	30%
Total	106	100%

Additional narrative responses: 74

Appendix A

10. Please indicate all of the resources you used to handle your emotional responses to change and to learn skills to constructively deal with professional changes. *(Note: We are not inquiring about how you learned new skills required for you to perform as a teacher, but rather, how you learned to adjust to the different norms and feelings that emerge when you—or the things around you—change.)*

Individual or group counseling	32	29%
Courses, workshops, or conference sessions	74	67%
Books or journal articles	60	55%
Talking informally with other teachers	103	94%
Talking with family and friends who aren't teachers	70	64%
Other, please briefly describe:	25	23%

11. Have you had an opportunity, as a teacher, to make use of something you've learned through an experience with change in your personal life?

Yes	82	81%
No	19	19%
Total	101	100%

Additional narrative responses: 80

12. Many of the skills needed to manage and lead change are ones teachers use to manage classrooms and lead students to learning, such as the ones identified below by Berliner. Please indicate which of the following "executive functions of teaching" you use on a regular basis.

Planning	102	96%
Communicating goals	93	88%
Regulating the work flow	78	74%
Creating a pleasant environment	104	98%
Educating new members to the work group	76	72%
Relating the work of the site to other units in the system	54	51%
Supervising and collaborating with others	91	86%
Motivating those being supervised	67	63%
Evaluating the performance of those being supervised	44	42%

13. Have you initiated a change within your own classroom that impacted your life as a teacher? Examples include developing new ways to involve family members or

community volunteers, seeking out new approaches to instruction, and volunteering for a new grade level or teaching partnership.

Yes	88	85%
No	15	15%
Total	103	100%

Additional narrative responses: 84

14. Have you initiated a change that was intended to have an impact on the broader school community? Examples include advocating for a new approach to curriculum and instruction or to school organization, organizing professional development opportunities for teachers, and establishing new clubs or services for students.

Yes	69	68%
No	33	32%
Total	102	100%

Additional narrative responses: 69

15. Are there specific changes you anticipate making in your teaching career in the next five years?

Yes	55	55%
No	45	45%
Total	100	100%

Additional narrative responses: 59

16. What suggestions would you provide to help teachers undertake change in their professional lives?

Narrative responses: 101

17. Please provide any additional observations which could help the authors enable teachers to make the best use of changes throughout their careers.

Narrative responses: 71

18. Please identify all roles that you have taken in school settings during your teaching career.

General education teacher	75	69%
Coteacher	74	68%
Special education teacher—inclusion specialist	35	32%

Special education teacher—resource room	33	30%
Special education teacher—self-contained	41	38%
Mentor to new or struggling teachers	77	71%
Department head or team leader	39	36%
Supervisor of teachers in your own building	13	12%
Assistant principal	1	1%
Principal	3	3%
Supervisor of teachers in training (undergrad or grad students)	41	38%
Other: please describe:	33	30%

19. Please indicate all the different types of districts in which you have worked as an educator for at least a year of full-time teaching.

Urban	41	38%
Suburban	68	62%
Rural	67	61%
Private	23	21%
Religious-affiliation	10	9%
Other, please describe	12	11%

The following debriefing questions will help us to assess our survey. Thank you for responding to them.

20. If you had answered these questions a month ago, how different might your answers have been?

Very different	1	1%
Neutral	2	2%
Very similar	104	97%
Total	107	100%

21. How difficult was it for you to respond to the questions in this survey?

Difficult	4	4%
Neutral	25	23%
Easy	78	73%
Total	107	100%

22. Were one or more of the questions in this survey upsetting to you?

Yes	4	4%
Not sure	6	6%
No	96	91%
Total	106	100%

Appendix B

Interview Questions

Introductory Comments: Thank you for your willingness to participate in this phone interview. Please be assured that you will have complete confidentiality in the responses you provide. We have no way to connect your interview answers to your survey answers. We will make sure to disguise any responses you provide before they are included in our book.

1. I'd like to ask you to think about a major change you experienced as a teacher. Can you describe the change and its outcome briefly?

2. I'm interested in learning about how you experienced the **process** of change. What did you think, feel, and do as you were adjusting to the change?
   - Were there noticeable stages to your response?
   - What strategies did you use to help you manage the change?
   - Did you come to see the value or importance of the change differently over time?
   - In hindsight, is there anything you would have done differently?

3. Can you recall a time when you resisted a change?
   - If yes,
     - What effect did your resistance have?
     - If you had it to do over, would you change the way you responded?

4. Teachers are often perceived as resistant to change. Is that a fair characterization?
   - If yes, why do teachers often resist change?
   - If no, why does the perception persist?

5. In what ways has change been beneficial for you and your students? In what ways, if any, has it been harmful?

6. Please tell me about a time when you decided to undertake a change effort. This might have been a change you could make on your own, or one that required you to bring others along.
   - What strategies did you use to promote the change?
   - Were the outcomes what you expected?
   - What made the effort a success? (a disappointment?)

7. What obstacles have you faced in adapting to change?
   - Were you able to overcome them? How?

8. We're trying to learn if teachers experience change throughout their entire careers, or if some stages are more likely to be characterized by change than others.
   - Have the changes you've experienced been spread across most of your career thus far, or have they been clustered?
   - Are there some changes all teachers should attempt at some point in their careers?

9. As you look back at your career, which events or developments stand out as milestones?

10. What advice do you have for teachers who are struggling with change?

11. Have you observed or experienced a failure to make a needed change? What were the consequences?

Thank you very much for your participation. Do you have any questions for me?

Appendix C

Professional Organizations for Teachers

Teachers can benefit enormously from membership in professional organizations. Good organizations create a variety of ways for members to connect with others who share their interests and face similar challenges. Newsletters keep members up to date on emerging trends and political developments that affect them. Journals allow teachers to stay abreast of current best practices in curriculum and instruction, often disseminating ideas for unit and lesson plans. Annual conferences offer teachers rich opportunities for professional development. Below are some well-respected professional organizations for teachers; there is sure to be one that you will find helpful. Web searches will lead you to other groups set up for teachers; be aware that some are commercial endeavors established for the purpose of making a profit. Nonprofit groups whose primary mission is service to teachers typically are designated by ".org" rather than ".com". You can check the organization's "About Us" and "Our Mission" pages for more information.

For All Educators

Phi Delta Kappa (PDK)
www.pdkintl.org

Association for Supervision and Curriculum Development (ASCD)
www.ascd.org

National School Reform Faculty
www.nsrfharmony.org

National Parent and Teacher Association
www.pta.org

Groups With a Content Specialization

Literacy and English Language Arts

International Reading Association (IRA)
www.reading.org

National Council of Teachers of English (NCTE)
www.ncte.org

Second Language Literacy

Teachers of English to Students of Other Languages (TESOL)
www.tesol.org

National Association for Bilingual Education (NABE)
www.nabe.org

Social Studies

National Council for the Social Studies (NCSS)
www.socialstudies.org

National Council for Geographic Education
www.ncge.org

Science

National Science Teachers Association (NSTA)
www.nsta.org

American Association of Physics Teachers (AAPT)
www.aapt.org

National Middle Level Science Teachers Association (NMLSTA)
www.nmlsta.org

Math

National Council of Teachers of Mathematics (NCTM)
www.nctm.org

Engineering

American Society for Engineering Education (ASEE)
www.asee.org

The Arts

National Art Education Association (NAEA)
www.naea-reston.org

Music Teachers National Association (MTNA)
www.mtna.org

American Alliance for Health, Physical Education, Recreation, and Dance (AAHPERD)
www.aahperd.org

Foreign Language

American Council on the Teaching of Foreign Languages (ACTFL)
www.actfl.org

Health and Physical Education

American Alliance for Health, Physical Education, Recreation, and Dance (AAHPERD)
www.aahperd.org

Sexuality Information & Education Council of the United States (SIECUS)
www.siecus.org

Appendix C

Organizations With a Focus on Particular Student Groups

National Association for the Education of Young Children (NAEYC)
www.naeyc.org

National Middle School Association (NMSA)
www.nmsa.org

National Alliance of Black School Educators (NABSE)
www.nabse.org

Council for Exceptional Children (CEC)
www.cec.sped.org

American Council on Rural Special Education (ACRES)
www.acres-sped.org

National Association for Gifted Children (NAGC)
www.nagc.org

Gay, Lesbian and Straight Education Network (GLSEN)
www.glsen.org

Teachers Using Technology

International Society for Technology in Education (ISTE)
www.iste.org

Computer-Using Educators (CUE)
www.cue.org

Teacher Unions

National Education Association (NEA)
www.nea.org

American Federation of Teachers (AFT)
www.aft.org

Other

National Staff Development Council (NSDC)
www.nsdc.org

National Association of Independent Schools (NAIS)
www.nais.org

North American Montessori Teachers' Association (NAMTA)
www.Montessori-namta.org

References

Adams, J. E. (2000). *Taking charge of curriculum: Teacher networks and curriculum implementation.* New York: Teachers College Press.

Adelman, H. S., & Taylor, L. (2007). Systematic change for school improvement. *Journal of Educational and Psychological Consultation, 17*(1), 55–77.

Alger, C. L. (2007). Engaging student teachers' hearts and minds in the struggle to address (il)literacy in content area classrooms. *Journal of Adolescent and Adult Literacy, 50*(8), 620–630.

Bascia, N., & Hargreaves, A. (2000). Teaching and leading on the sharp edge of change. In N. Bascia & A. Hargreaves (Eds.), *The sharp edge of educational change: Teaching, leading and the realities of reform* (pp. 3–26). London: Routledge Falmer.

Berliner, D. C. (1983). The executive functions of teaching. *Instructor, 93*(2), 29–39.

Berliner, D. C. (1990). If the metaphor fits, why not wear it? The teacher as executive. *Theory into Practice, 29* (2), 85–93.

Berliner, D. C., & Biddle, B. J. (1996). *The manufactured crisis: Myths, fraud, and the attack on America's public schools.* New York: Basic Books.

Bolman, L. G., & Deal, T. E. (2008). *Reframing organizations: Artistry, choice and leadership* (4th ed.). San Francisco: Jossey-Bass.

Bouquillon, E. A., Sosik, J. J., & Lee, D. (2005). 'It's only a phase': Examining trust, identification and mentoring functions received across the mentoring phases. *Mentoring & Tutoring: Partnership in Learning, 1*(2), 239–258.

Bridges, W. (2004). *Transitions: Making sense of life's changes* (2nd ed.). Cambridge, MA: Da Capo Press.

Brown, J. L., & Moffett, C. A. (1999). *The hero's journey: How educators can transform schools and improve learning.* Alexandria, VA: Association for Supervision & Curriculum Development.

Bullough, R. V. (1997). Becoming a teacher: Self and the social location of teacher education. In B. J. Biddle, T. L. Good & I. F. Goodson (Eds.), *International handbook of teachers and teaching* (pp. 79–134). Dordrecht, The Netherlands: Kluwer Academic.

Burstein, N., Sears, S., Wilcoxen, S., Cabello, B., & Spagna, M. (2004). Moving toward inclusive practices. *Remedial and Special Education, 24*(2), 104–116.

Cherry, D., & Spiegel, J. (2006). *Leadership, myth & metaphor: Finding common ground to guide effective school change.* Thousand Oaks, CA: Corwin.

Cochran-Smith, M. (2005). The politics of teacher education and the curse of complexity. *The Journal of Teacher Education, 56* (3), 181–185.

Collinson, V., Cook, T. F., & Conley, S. (2006). Organizational learning in schools and school systems: Improving learning, teaching and leading. *Theory into Practice, 45*(2), 107–116.

Craig, C. J. 2001. Relationships between and among teacher knowledge, communities of knowing, and top-down school reform: A case of "The Monkey's Paw." *Curriculum Inquiry, 301*(1), 303–331.

Craig, C. J. 2006. Musings on the margin: Curriculum and teaching in an age of school *reform. Curriculum and Teaching Dialogue, 8* (1/2), 3–14.

Cramer, S. F. (2006). *The special educator's guide to collaboration: Improving relationships with co-teachers, teams, and families* (2nd ed.). Thousand Oaks, CA: Corwin.

Cuban, L. (1988). *The managerial imperative and the practice of leadership in schools.* Albany, NY: State University of New York Press.

Cuban, L. (1992). Curriculum stability and change. In P. Jackson (Ed.), *Handbook of research on curriculum* (pp. 216–247). New York: Macmillan.

Cuban, L. (2004). *The blackboard and the bottom line: Why schools can't be businesses.* Cambridge, MA: Harvard University Press.

Cuban, L. (2007, March 28). The never-ending quest: Lessons learned from urban school reform. *Education Week, 26* (29), 26.

Danielson, C. (2006). *Teacher leadership that strengthens professional practice.* Alexandria, VA: Association for Supervision and Curriculum Development.

Day, C. (2002). The challenge to be the best: Reckless curiosity and mischievous motivation. *Teachers & Teaching, 8*(3/4), 421–434.

Donovan, L., Hartley, K., & Strudler, N. (2007). Teacher concerns during initial implementation of a one-to-one laptop initiative at the middle school level. *Journal of Research on Technology in Education, 39*(3), 263–286.

Easton, L. B. (2008). From professional development to professional learning. *Phi Delta Kappan, 89*(10), 755–761.

Evans, R. (2001). *The human side of school change: Reform, resistance, and the real-life problems of innovation.* San Francisco: Jossey-Bass.

Faust, D. G. (2008). *This republic of suffering: Death and the American Civil War.* New York: Knopf.

Ferrero, D. J. (2006). Having it all. *Educational Leadership, 63*(6), 8–14.

Foley, J. (1993). *An examination of how elementary administrators help teachers change their beliefs about teaching mathematics and guide the process of reform.* (ERIC Document Reproduction Service No. ED372925). Retrieved September 14, 2008, from http://www.eric.ed.gov/ERICDocs/data/ericdocs2sql/content_storage_01/0000019b/80/16/1c/14.pdf

Fullan, M. G. (1994). Coordinating top-down and bottom-up strategies for educational reform. In *Systemic reform—Perspectives on personalizing education.* Retrieved September 14, 2008, from http://www.ed.gov/pubs/EdReformStudies/SysReforms/fullan1.html

Fullan, M. (2001). *Leading in a culture of change.* San Francisco: Jossey-Bass.

Fuller, F. F. (1969). Concerns of teachers: A developmental conceptualization. *American Educational Research Journal, 6*(2), 207–226.

Fuller, F. F., & Brown, O. H. (1975). *Becoming a teacher: Teacher education 1975.* Chicago: The National Society for the Study of Education.

Gay, G. (2000). *Culturally responsive teaching: Theory, research, and practice.* New York: Teachers College Press.

Gregory, T. B., & Smith, G. R. (1987). *High schools as communities: The small school reconsidered.* Bloomington, IN: Phi Delta Kappa Educational Foundation.

Guskey, T. R. (2002). Professional development and teacher change. *Teachers & Teaching, 8*(3/4), 381–391.

Hall, G. E., & Hord, S. (2001). *Implementing change: Patterns, principles, and potholes.* Boston: Allyn & Bacon.

Hall, G. E., & Hord, S. M. (2006). *Implementing change: Patterns, principles and potholes* (2nd ed.). Boston, MA: Allyn & Bacon.

Hanson, S., & Moir, E. (2008). Beyond mentoring: Influencing the professional practice and careers of experienced teachers. *Phi Delta Kappan, 89*(6), 453–458.

Hargreaves, A. (1994). *Changing teachers, changing time: Teachers' work and culture in the postmodern age.* London: Cassell.

Hargreaves, A. (1998). The emotional practice of teaching. *Teaching and Teacher Education, 14*(8), 835–854.

Hargreaves, A. (2000). Four ages of professionalism and professional learning. *Teachers and Teaching: History and Practice, 6*(2), 151–182.

Hargreaves, A. (2005). Educational change takes ages: Life, career and generational factors in teachers' emotional responses to educational change. *Teaching and Teacher Education, 21*(8), 967–983.

Hargreaves, A., Earl, L., Moore, S., & Manning, S. (2001). *Learning to change.* San Francisco: Jossey-Bass.

Hargreaves, A., & Fullan, M. (1998). *What's worth fighting for in education?* London: Taylor & Francis.

Havelock, R. G., & Hamilton, J. L. (2004). *Guiding change in special education: How to help schools with new ideas and practices.* Thousand Oaks, CA: Corwin.

References

Hohn, M. D. (1998). *Why is change so hard?* Retrieved September 14, 2008, from http://www.ncsall.net/?id=771&pid=396

Huberman, M. (1995). Professional careers and professional development. In T. R. Guskey & M. Huberman (Eds.), *Professional development in education: New paradigms and practices* (pp. 192–224). New York: Teachers College Press.

Huberman, A. M., Grounauer, M., & Marti, J. (1993). *The lives of teachers.* New York: Teachers College Press.

Huberman, A. M., & Miles, A. B. (1984). *Innovation up close: How school improvement works.* New York: Plenum.

Interstate New Teacher Assessment and Support Consortium (INTASC). (1992). *Model standards for beginning teachers licensing and development: A resource for state dialogue.* Washington, DC: Council of Chief State School Officers.

Intrator, S. M., & Kunzman, R. (2006). Starting with the soul. *Educational Leadership, 63*(6), 38–42.

Jersild, A. T. (2003). *When teachers face themselves.* Temecula, CA: Textbook Publishers.

Jick, T. D., & Peiperl, M. (2003). *Managing change: Cases and concepts* (2nd ed.). New York: McGraw-Hill/Irwin.

Johnson, S. M. (2001). Can professional certification for teachers reshape teaching as a career? *Phi Delta Kappan, 82*(5), 393–398.

Johnson, S. M., Birkeland, S. E., Donaldson, M. L., Kardos, S. M., Kauffman, D., Liu, E., & Peske, H. G. (2004). *Finders and keepers: Helping new teachers survive and thrive in our schools.* San Francisco: Jossey-Bass.

Karby, S. (2006). *Reforming teacher education: Something old, something new.* Santa Monica, CA: RAND Education.

Kilgallon, P., Maloney, C., & Lock, G. (2008). Early childhood teachers coping with educational change. *Australian Journal of Early Childhood, 33*(1), 23–29.

Langley, D. J., O'Connor, T. W., & Welkener, M. M. (2004). A transformative model for designing professional development activities. In C. M. Wehlburg & S. Chadwick-Blossey (Eds.), *To improve the academy: Resources for faculty, instructional and organizational development: Vol. 22* (pp. 145–155). Bolton, MA: Anker.

Lewis, C., Perry, R., Hurd, J., & O'Connell, M. (2006). Lesson study comes of age in North America. *Phi Delta Kappan, 88*(4), 273–281.

Lieberman, A., & Miller, L. (1999). *Teachers—Transforming their world and their work.* New York: Teachers College Press.

Lipstein, O. (2007, August). Beacon's Hot. *Inside Out Hudson Valley,* 50–52.

Little, J. W. (1990). The persistence of privacy: Autonomy and initiative in teachers' professional relations. *Teachers College Record, 91*(4), 509–536.

Little, J. W. (2001). Professional development in pursuit of school reform. In A. Lieberman & L. Miller (Eds.), *Teachers caught in the action: Professional development that matters* (pp. 28–44). NY: Teachers College Press.

Little, J. W., & Bartlett, L. (2002). Career and commitment in the context of comprehensive school reform. *Teachers and Teaching: Theory and Practice, 8*(3/4), 345–354.

Lopez-Real, F., & Kwan, T. (2005). Mentors' perceptions of their own professional development during mentoring. *Journal of Education for Teaching, 31*(1), 15–24.

Lortie, D. C. (2002; 1975). *Schoolteacher: A sociological study (with a new preface).* Chicago: University of Chicago Press.

Lowney, C. (2003). *Heroic leadership: Best practices from a 450-year-old company that changed the world.* Chicago: Loyola Press.

Mandel, S. (2006). What new teachers really need. *Educational Leadership, 63*(6), 66–69.

Marshak, D. (1996). The emotional experience of school change: Resistance, loss, and grief. *NASSP Bulletin, 80*(577), 72–77.

Martin, B. (2007). Teacher leaders: qualities and roles. *Journal for Quality & Participation, 30*(4), 17–18.

Masci, F. J., Cuddapah, J. L., & Pajak, E. F. (2008). Becoming an agent of stability: Keeping your school in balance during the perfect storm. *American Secondary Education, 36*(2), 57–68.

McLaughlin, M. W., Pfeifer, R. S., Swanson-Owens, D., & Yee, S. (1986). Why teachers won't teach. *Phi Delta Kappan, 67*(6), 420–426.

McLaughlin, M. W., & Talbert, J. E. (2001). *Professional communities and the work of high school teaching* (1st ed.). University of Chicago Press.

McNess, E., Broadfoot, P., & Osborn, M. (2003). Is the effective compromising the affective? *British Educational Research Journal, 29*(2), 243–257.

Meister, D., & Nolan, J. (2001). Out on a limb on our own. *Teachers College Record, 103*(4), 608–634.

Mohr, N., & Dichter, A. (2001). Building a learning organization. *Phi Delta Kappan, 82*(10), 744–747.

Move me on. (2008). *Teaching History, 30,* 52–55.

National Council of Teachers of Mathematics. *Why advocate?* Retrieved March 20, 2008, from http://www.nctm.org/news/content.aspx?id=490

Orr, J. N. (2000). Change is not transition. *Computer-Aided Engineering, 19*(6), 66.

Pedro, J. Y. (2005). Reflection in teacher education: Exploring pre-service teachers' meanings of reflective practice. *Reflective Practice, 6*(1), 49–66.

Pickering, A. M. (2006). Learning about university teaching: Reflections on a research study investigating influences for change. *Teaching in Higher Education, 11*(3), 319–335.

Quinn, R. E. (1996). *Deep change: Discovering the leader within.* San Francisco: Jossey-Bass.

Ragland, M. A., Asera, R., & Johnson, J. F., Jr. (1999). *Urgency, responsibility, and efficacy: Preliminary findings of a study of high-performing Texas school districts.* Austin, TX: The Charles A. Dana Center, The University of Texas at Austin.

Rallis, S. F., & Rossman, G. B. (with Phlegar, J. M., & Abeille, A.). (1995). *Dynamic teachers: Leaders of change.* Thousand Oaks, CA: Corwin.

Ramsey, R. D. (1999). *Lead, follow, or get out of the way: How to be a more effective leader in today's schools.* Thousand Oaks, CA: Corwin.

Reeves, D. (2006). Pull the weeds before you plant the flowers. *Educational Leadership, 64*(1), 89–90.

Richards, J. C. (2000, July). Exploring how teachers change. *The Language Teacher Online, 24*(07). Retrieved September 14, 2008, from http://www.jalt-publications.org/tlt/articles/2000/07/richards

Richards, J. (2002). Why teachers resist change (and what principals can do about it). *Principal, 81*(4), 74–77.

Richardson, V. (1998, September). How teachers change. *Focus on basics: Connecting research and practice, 2*(C), 1. Retrieved September 14, 2008, from http://www.ncsall.net/?id=395

Richardson, V., & Placier, P. (2001). Teacher change. In V. Richardson (Ed.), *Handbook of research on teaching* (pp. 905–947). Washington, DC: American Educational Research Association.

Roettger, C. (2006). Change from the heart. *The Journal for Quality and Participation, 29*(2), 18–21.

Rogers, E. M. (1995). *Diffusion of innovations* (4th ed.). New York: Simon & Schuster.

Schmoker, M. (1999). *Results: The key to continuous school improvement.* Alexandria, VA: Association for Supervision and Curriculum Development.

Seaton, M., Emmett, R. E., Welsh, K., & Petrossian, A. (2008). Teaming up for teaching and learning. *Leadership, 37*(3), 26–29.

Senge, P. M. (1990). *The fifth discipline: The art and practice of the learning organization.* New York: Currency/Doubleday.

Sergiovanni, T. J. (2000). *The lifeworld of leadership: Creating culture, community, and personal meaning in our schools.* San Francisco: Jossey-Bass.

Sindelar, P. T., Shearer, D. K., Yendol-Hoppey, D., & Liebert, T. W. (2006). The sustainability of inclusive school reform. *Exceptional Children, 72*(3), 317–331.

Smith, N., Petty, T., & Day, B. (2008). The bare necessities: A look at the current needs of teachers. *Delta Kappa Gamma Bulletin, 74*(4), 29–33.

Stiegelbauer, S. M. (1994). Change has changed: Implications for implementation of assessments from the organizational change literature. In *Systemic reform—Perspectives on personalizing education.* Retrieved September 14, 2008, from http://www.ed.gov/pubs/EdReformStudies/SysReforms/stiege11.html

References

Stipek, D. (2006). Accountability comes to preschool: Can we make it work for young children? *Phi Delta Kappan, 87*(10), 740–747.

Thompson, N., & Hammer, M. (2007). Weaving gold: Transitioning nursing practice from a medical model to a nursing model. *Oncology Nursing Forum, 34*(2), 483.

Vavasseur, C. B., & MacGregor, S. K. (2008). Extending content-focused professional development through online communities of practice. *Journal of Research on Technology in Education, 40*(4), 517–536.

Wagner, T. (2001). Leadership for learning: An action theory of school change. *Phi Delta Kappan, 82*(5), 378–383.

Waks, L. J. (2007). The concept of fundamental educational change. *Educational Theory, 57*(3), 277–295.

Watson, D. L., & Tharp, R. G. (1977). *Self-directed behavior: Self-modification for personal adjustment* (2nd ed.). Monterey, CA: Brooks/Cole.

Zimmerman, J. (2006). Why some teachers resist change and what principals can do about it. *National Association of Secondary School Principals Bulletin, 90*(3), 238–249.

Index

Index

Index

CORWIN

A SAGE Company

The Corwin logo—a raven striding across an open book—represents the union of courage and learning. Corwin is committed to improving education for all learners by publishing books and other professional development resources for those serving the field of PreK–12 education. By providing practical, hands-on materials, Corwin continues to carry out the promise of its motto: **"Helping Educators Do Their Work Better."**